DISCOVERING YOUR GOD-GIVEN POTENTALS:
Unleashing Your True Purpose

Akinbowale Isaac Adewumi

Copyright © 2024 Akinbowale Isaac Adewumi
DISCOVERING YOUR GOD-GIVEN POTENTALS: UNLEASHING YOUR TRUE PURPOSE

ISBN: 978-1-989746-12-7

All rights reserved
No part of this publication may be reproduced, stored in a retrieval system or transmitted in any form or by any means, electronic, mechanical, photocopying, recording or otherwise, without prior written permission of the copyright owner.

Unless otherwise indicated, Scripture quotations are taken from the HOLY BIBLE, King James Version (KJV)

Formatting and Editing:
Taiwo Solomon Adeodu: +2348108673939

DEDICATION

"Every good gift and every perfect gift is from above, and cometh down from the Father of lights, with whom is no variableness, neither shadow of turning." (James 1:17).

Dedicated to all sincere seekers of true wealth.

PREFACE

Every individual is uniquely endowed with talents and gifts by God, intended for a divine purpose. Just as the body of Christ comprises diverse members, each with distinct roles, yet indispensable to the whole, our varied talents collectively serve to advance the Kingdom of God and our well-being on earth. In 1 Corinthians 12, Paul illustrates this analogy, likening believers to different parts of the body, all essential for its proper functioning.

Likewise, our diverse talents, though distinct, contribute to the greater purpose when utilized for God's glory. Some may readily discern their talents, others may seek guidance. Through prayer, as instructed in Matthew 7:7, we can seek God's guidance in discovering our gifts. Seeking input from others and reflecting on our passions also illuminate our unique abilities.

Furthermore, honing our talents demands dedication and practice. Even those gifted naturally must cultivate their skills to be faithful stewards of God's blessings. As emphasized in 1 Peter 4:10-11, we are called to employ our gifts to serve one another, thereby glorifying God through our actions.

Whether in speaking, ministering or any other pursuit, utilizing our talents for God's purposes enriches our lives with significance and enables us to share His love. Let us therefore embrace our gifts with gratitude and commitment, recognizing them as instruments for fulfilling God's divine plan.

There are numerous opportunities to glorify God through the use of our talents. For instance, if you possess the gift of teaching, you can impart knowledge and wisdom by leading a Sunday school class at your church. Artists can express their creativity by producing pieces that reflect biblical truths or resonate with people's hearts. If you excel in interpersonal communication, reaching out to lonely individuals for companionship can demonstrate God's love and compassion. Likewise, those skilled in culinary arts can provide comfort and sustenance to those in need, such as bereaved individuals.

In our daily lives, we must remain vigilant for opportunities to serve God and employ our gifts. The manifestation of using our talents for God's glory may vary from day to day. On some days, we may clearly discern God's work through our actions, at other times, it may be more subtle, occurring behind closed doors without our immediate awareness of its impact on others.

Even when we cannot perceive the direct influence of our talents, it is crucial to remain obedient to God's calling, for our actions may profoundly impact someone's life without our knowledge. As Matthew 5:16 reminds us, our good works should shine brightly before others, ultimately glorifying our Heavenly Father.

If you find yourself feeling discontented or out of place, it could be a prompting from God indicating that you are meant for a different purpose. Just as a fish out of water struggles and suffocates, prolonged dissatisfaction may signal that you are in the wrong environment. Pay heed to the whispers of your God-given gifts, passions and the counsel of others, as they may guide you toward a more fulfilling path aligned with God's will..

Society often portrays dissatisfaction as something to be avoided at all costs, urging us to suppress it or disguise it with temporary fixes. However, this perspective overlooks the possibility that God may use dissatisfaction as a catalyst for change, nudging us toward a path where our talents can flourish.

It's true that dissatisfaction can sometimes stem from spiritual warfare, as Ephesians 6:10-12 warns us, it can also serve as a gentle prompting from God, indicating that He has a different purpose in mind for us. Therefore, if you find yourself persistently discontented in your current career or job, despite earnest prayer, seeking counsel and consulting Scripture, it may be a signal that God has another plan awaiting your embrace.

Rather than resigning ourselves to enduring misery as a form of "bearing our cross," we should prayerfully consider whether God is using our dissatisfaction to steer us toward a more fulfilling path. Embracing this discomfort with openness to God's leading can ultimately lead to a deeper alignment with His will and a more abundant life lived in accordance with our God-given gifts and purpose.

In our journey of discerning God's purpose for our lives, we encounter various signals and affirmations from both within and without. Just as dissatisfaction can sometimes serve as a gentle prod from God, so too can the observations and insights of those around us.

Scripture reminds us in Proverbs 11:14 that "Where no counsel is, the people fall: but in the multitude of counsellors there is safety." Seeking counsel from trusted individuals who are grounded in faith can offer valuable perspectives on our gifts and talents. When multiple voices resonate with what we already sense within ourselves, our passions, convictions and the direction we believe God is leading us, it can serve as a confirmation of our God-given purpose. However, discernment is crucial. Not all feedback is aligned with God's plan for us. We must filter external input through the lens of Scripture and prayer, examining whether it harmonizes with God's Word and our relationship with Him.

Ultimately, when others affirm our gifts and talents in ways that align with God's revealed will, it can be a powerful affirmation of our calling. It signals that God may be using them as vessels to speak truth into our lives, guiding us toward a deeper understanding of how we can serve Him effectively.

Therefore, let us heed the wise counsel of others, recognizing it as a potential avenue through which God communicates His purpose for us. By remaining grounded in prayer, Scripture and the guidance of the Holy Spirit, we can navigate the complexities of discernment with clarity and confidence, ultimately fulfilling our God-given destiny.

Just as you recognize that your strengths lie in areas like writing, painting, drawing, singing, and communication, Scripture teaches us that God endows each of us with diverse gifts for His purposes.

In 1 Corinthians 12, Paul discusses the concept of spiritual gifts, likening them to various parts of the body. Just as the body is composed of different parts with distinct functions, so too are believers equipped with different gifts to serve the body of Christ effectively. You may not excel in mathematics, your proficiency in writing, painting, and other creative endeavours showcases the unique talents God has bestowed upon you. These gifts serve as road signs guiding you toward the path God has prepared for you.

Indeed, self-reflection and assessment of our talents and interests can provide valuable insights into our God-given purpose. By identifying areas where we excel and what activities bring us joy, we gain clarity on how God may be calling us to serve Him.

Moreover, your analogy of "Gift Seeds" is reminiscent of Jesus' parable of the talents in Matthew 25:14-30. In this parable, the master entrusts his servants with talents (a form of currency), expecting them to invest and multiply what they have been given. Similarly, God expects us to cultivate and utilize the gifts He has bestowed upon us for His glory and the benefit of others.

Exploring new interests and experiences can indeed reveal more about our God-given talents and passions. As we step out in faith and engage in diverse activities, God often unveils hidden talents and opportunities for service, further illuminating His purpose for our lives.

Therefore, let us embrace the unique gifts God has given us, using them faithfully to glorify Him and contribute to His Kingdom work. Through prayer, self-reflection and willingness to explore new avenues, we can discover and fulfill our God-given purpose with joy and confidence.

Your reflections on what stirs your emotions and passions resonate deeply with the biblical understanding of God's calling and purpose for our lives. Just as you discern how certain issues and experiences evoke anger, joy, excitement or passion within you, Scripture teaches us to pay attention to the movements of our hearts as potential indicators of our God-given purpose.

Your righteous indignation at the godless condition of the world and your compassion for the vulnerable, such as abused children, reflect the heart of God for justice and mercy. Conversely, your deep appreciation for stories of loyal love and the power of well-crafted words mirror God's heart for redemption and communication.

As you recognize the intersection of your talents and passions, you discern a calling toward written and spoken communication that touches people on a spiritual and emotional level. This aligns with biblical principles of using our gifts and passions to glorify God and edify others, as exemplified by figures like the prophets, apostles and writers of Scripture.

Indeed, prayerful reflection and seeking God's guidance are essential in discerning our purpose. By asking God to reveal the things that move us deeply and making a list of these insights, we open ourselves to His leading and direction.

Furthermore, recognizing that our purpose is not merely about ourselves, but about what God wants to accomplish through us underscores the biblical truth of being vessels for His Kingdom work. By ignoring or neglecting the signs of our purpose, whether through dissatisfaction, affirmations from others or the stirring of our passions, we risk missing out on the joy and fulfillment of walking in God's intended plan for our lives.

However, we can trust in God's faithfulness to reveal His purpose to us as we diligently seek Him. Hebrews 11:6 reminds us that God rewards those who earnestly seek Him, assuring us that He is fully capable of unveiling His purpose for our lives in His perfect timing.

Therefore, let us continue to seek God fervently, trusting in His guidance and provision as we embark on the journey of discovering and fulfilling our God-given purpose for His glory and the benefit of others.

CONTENTS

Title page

Dedication

Preface

1. Introduction
2. Cultivating a Strong Relationship with God
3. Understanding Your God-given Potentials
4. Leveraging Your Unique Talents and Abilities
5. Overcoming Limiting Benefits and Self-Doubt
6. Seeking God's Guidance and Direction
7. Discovering Your Passion and Purpose
8. Developing a Growth Mindset
9. Setting Clear and Meaningful Goals
10. Taking Bold Steps and Embracing Challenges
11. Growing Resilience and Perseverance
12. Harvesting the Power of Faith and Prayer
13. Surrounding Yourself with Positive Influence
14. Overcoming Obstacles and Adversities
15. Stepping Out of Your Comfort Zone
16. Developing a Positive Self-Image
17. Nurturing Your Spiritual Gifts

18. Fostering Your Talents: A Spiritual Journey

19. Realizing Your Core Value

20. Living a Life of Integrity and Purpose

21. Making Wise and Godly Decisions

22. Maximizing Your Time and Resources

23. Building Healthy Relationships

24. Engendering Continuous Learning and Personal Growth

25. Celebrating Your Achievements and Milestones

26. Leaving a Lasting Legacy

27. Overcoming Fear and Taking Calculated Risks

28. Maintaining Balance and Prioritizing Self-Care

29. Achieving Life Balance: Placing Priority on Self-Care and Well-Being

30. Accepting Support: Overcoming Stigma and Seeking Help

31. Embracing Change and Adaptability

32. Curating a Spirit of Gratitude and Thankfulness

33. Staying Focused and Determined on Your Journey

34. Conclusion: Living Your God-Given Potential

Epilogue

References

1

Introduction

In the vast tapestry of existence, everyone is woven with a unique blend of talents, passions and experiences, meticulously crafted by the hand of the Creator. Yet, amid the complexities of life, many find themselves adrift, yearning for a deeper sense of purpose and fulfillment. It is within this yearning that the journey of discovering one's God-given potential begins.

Discovering Your God-Given Potential: Unleashing Your True Purpose is not merely a book; it is a roadmap, a guide that navigates the winding paths of self-discovery and spiritual discernment. It is an invitation to embark on a transformative journey, one that unveils the mysteries of God's design for your life and empowers you to walk confidently in your true calling.

Why are we so consumed with the quest for purpose? Is there truly a divine calling for each of us and if so, how can we uncover it? Do we walk a path preordained by God or do we shape our purpose through our own choices? What leads to a profound and enduring sense of fulfillment and contentment? How do we define "success" in the grand scheme of life and how can it be quantified? These fundamental inquiries echo throughout the ages, resonating within the depths of every human soul.

Indeed, the desire to live a life of significance, to leave a positive impact on the world, is inherent in the human experience. Nearly all individuals yearn for a purpose that transcends mere survival and fleeting pleasures. Yet, amidst the clamour of hedonistic pursuits and selfish endeavours, many are awakening to the emptiness of lives devoid of lasting value. This awakening, questioning the essence of our existence, naturally leads to a pursuit of deeper meaning and purpose.

Throughout history, humanity has grappled with this existential longing, seeking answers in various forms. From the construction of monumental structures like pyramids and temples in ancient times to the modern-day investment in therapy, counseling and self-help programs, people from all walks of life have sought to decipher life's mysteries and uncover their true purpose.

However, amidst this quest for meaning, one enduring truth remains: true purpose is found in alignment with God's will and design for our lives. As we delve into the wisdom of Scripture and seek guidance from the Holy Spirit, we begin to discern the unique path God has laid out for us. It is through surrendering our will to His and embracing His divine plan that we find ultimate fulfillment and contentment.

Therefore, let us embark on this journey of discovery with humility and openness, trusting in God's guidance to reveal our purpose and empower us to live lives of significance and impact. As we align our hearts with His, may we find true success, not in worldly accolades or material wealth, but in fulfilling the purpose for which we were created and bringing glory to His name.

As we journey together through these pages, we will delve into the timeless wisdom of Scripture, drawing upon its rich tapestry of narratives, parables and teachings to illuminate the path before us. We will explore the intricate interplay between our talents, passions and the divine purposes woven into the fabric of our being.

However, this journey is not solely about introspection; it is also about action, about stepping boldly into the unique role that God has prepared for each of us. We will uncover practical strategies for discerning God's voice amidst the noise of life, for recognizing the signs and signals that point us toward our true purpose.

Moreover, we will confront the fears and doubts that often hinder our pursuit of God's calling, learning to embrace the discomfort of growth and change as we step into the fullness of who God created us to be.

"Discovering Your God-Given Potential" is a testament to the boundless love and grace of our Heavenly Father, Who intricately fashions each of us for a specific purpose, a purpose that is both unique and indispensable to His grand design. It is an affirmation that our lives are not accidents, but divine masterpieces, waiting to be unveiled and celebrated in all their splendor.

So, dear reader, as you embark on this journey of discovery, may you be filled with hope and anticipation, knowing that the God Who knit you together in your mother's womb is eager to reveal the fullness of your potential and guide you into the abundant life He has prepared for you.

Together, let us uncover the depths of our true purpose and unleash the extraordinary potential that lies within each of us.

2

Cultivating a Strong Relationship with God

The Almighty God cherishes you deeply and yearns for an intimate bond with you. Embracing the Lord with the entirety of your being, heart, soul, mind and strength, is not only a gracious invitation, but also a divine commandment. The Scriptures serve as a beacon of wisdom, illuminating the pathway toward fostering and fortifying this sacred relationship, guiding us to draw nearer to Him. Let us now explore the foundational truths from God's Word that illuminate the route to a profound connection with Him.

Accepting Jesus as Saviour: The foundation of our relationship with God begins with accepting Jesus as our Saviour. In John 14:6, Jesus declares Himself as the exclusive path to the Father. Through faith in Jesus and His sacrificial work on the cross, we receive forgiveness of sins and reconciliation with God. This acceptance opens the door to a profound relationship with Him.

Cultivating Intimacy through Prayer: Prayer serves as a vital channel for communication and communion with God. Following Jesus' example, we are encouraged to pray fervently, expressing our love, gratitude and desires to Him, while also listening for His guidance and direction (Matthew 6:9-13). Through prayer, we deepen our intimacy with God, drawing closer to Him in every aspect of our lives.

Studying and Meditating on God's Word: The Bible is God's revealed Word, providing us with invaluable insights into His character, His promises and His will for our lives. John 1:1, 14 reveals that Jesus Himself is the living Word. By immersing ourselves in Scripture, we come to know God more intimately and understand His divine purposes. As we meditate on His Word day and night, our love for Him grows deeper, and our relationship with Him flourishes.

Developing a Life of Obedience: Jesus emphasized the importance of obedience as an expression of love for God. In John 14:15, He states, *"If you love Me, you will keep My commandments."* As followers of Christ, we are called to align our lives with His teachings and live in obedience to His Word. Through obedience, we demonstrate our devotion to God and experience the richness of His presence in our lives. Just as Jesus exemplified perfect obedience to the Father, we strive to follow His example, knowing that our obedience deepens our love for God and strengthens our relationship with Him.

Depending on the Holy Spirit: In John 14:26, Jesus promised to send the Holy Spirit as a Helper and Guide to believers. The Holy Spirit dwells within us, empowering, guiding and transforming us into the image of Christ (Galatians 5:22-23). By depending on the Holy Spirit's guidance and allowing Him to work in us, our love for God deepens and we are enabled to live a life that honours Him.

Engaging in Worship and Praise: Worship is a powerful expression of love and adoration toward God. Jesus emphasized the importance of worshiping God in spirit and truth (John 4:23-24). Through worship and praise, our hearts are drawn closer to God and we enter into His presence, experiencing His love and grace in profound ways.

Seeking Fellowship with Other Believers: Hebrews 10:24-25 encourages us to gather with fellow believers for mutual support, encouragement and accountability. Being part of a community of believers strengthens our love for God and helps us grow in our relationship with Him as we participate in worship, fellowship and discipleship activities together.

Practicing Love for Others: Jesus taught that loving God and loving others are interconnected (John 13:34). By demonstrating love, forgiveness, kindness and compassion to others, we reflect God's love and deepen our relationship with Him. As we extend love to others, we embody the love of Christ and experience His presence in our lives.

Transformation and Witnessing: As we grow in our relationship with God, His transformative power works within us, shaping us into the image of Christ. 2 Corinthians 5:17 tells us that "... *if any man be in Christ, he is a new creature: old things are passed away; behold, all things are become new.*" This inner transformation is evident to others, serving as a powerful testimony to God's work in our lives. By embodying the love, grace and truth of Christ, we become effective witnesses, drawing others into relationship with Him.

Summarily, building a strong relationship with God involves accepting Jesus as our Saviour, repenting of our sins, studying the Scriptures, engaging in prayer, loving our neighbours, depending on the guidance of the Holy Spirit and faithfully obeying God's commands. Through these spiritual disciplines, we draw closer to God, experiencing His love, guidance and presence in profound ways. It's a lifelong journey of unwavering commitment and heartfelt desire to draw closer to God, knowing that as we invest in our relationship with Him, we will experience His love, favour, grace and transformative power in our lives.

3

Understanding Your God-Given Potentials

It is crucial for Christian men and women to grasp that their potentials originate from God and is bestowed upon them for His divine purpose. God, in His wisdom, assigns individuals specific identities to fulfill before endowing them with the gifts necessary to fulfill those identities. In the allocation of potential to God's people, the gifts infused with the initial identity are paramount and every gift bestowed by God serves a distinct purpose.

However, it is imperative to acknowledge that God's gifts surpass human imagination and comprehension. Contrary to common misconceptions, the verse in Matthew 7:11, *"If ye then, being evil, know how to give good gifts unto your children, how much more shall your Father which is in heaven give good things to them that ask him?"* refers to the gift of the Holy Spirit. Here, potential encompasses anything good and God's generosity far exceeds earthly standards.

Potential, in the spiritual sense, refers to the untapped and undeveloped abilities residing within individuals. While secular perspectives define potential as unrealized possibilities, Christian understanding emphasizes the importance of aligning one's potential with God's purpose. The key distinction between discovering and neglecting one's potential lies in comprehending and fulfilling one's God-given purpose.

To grasp the essence of potential, it is essential to identify its defining characteristics. Potential is not confined to past achievements, but involves surpassing previous accomplishments and experiencing continuous growth. It entails ongoing development, signifying the capacity for positive change and improvement in alignment with specific goals.

Additionally, potential encompasses future possibilities, reflecting the anticipation of further enhancement and advancement in God's sovereignty which empowers you to actively seek His will, courageously take steps of faith and earnestly pursue the opportunities He presents before you. It is essential to have unwavering faith that if God calls you to a task, He will equip you with everything necessary to fulfill it. Stepping out in faith is a pivotal aspect of realizing your God-given potential, as it demonstrates your trust in His provision and guidance.

Actualizing your God-given potential requires a deep alignment of your desires and actions with God's divine plan for your life. As believers, we are called to draw inspiration and guidance from the timeless wisdom of the Bible, allowing its teachings to illuminate our path toward purpose and fulfillment. By immersing ourselves in Scripture, we gain insight into God's character, His promises and His purposes, enabling us to navigate life's journey with confidence and conviction

Moreover, recognizing who you are in God and living according to His purposes is foundational to fulfilling your divine calling. The concept of "potential" can be understood in a profound biblical context. One definition of potential is "what you can do, but have not yet accomplished." A more spiritually insightful definition is:

Potential is how far you can go, not alone, but with God. Ephesians 3:20 says, *"Now unto him that is able to do exceeding abundantly above all that we ask or think, according to the power that worketh in us."*

God loves you immensely and has great expectations for your life. When you develop and utilize the gifts He has placed within you, regardless of how significant or insignificant they may seem, you are nurturing the potential He designed in you. This process is about aligning your abilities with God's purpose for you.

Your call is your personal spiritual direction, the specific plan God has for you to fulfill in His grand design. This call could manifest in various forms, such as evangelism, service, teaching or any unique path God has laid out for you. God delights in creativity and uniqueness; He created only one "you" and no one else can accomplish exactly what He has prepared for you.

Understanding your God-given potential involves:

Recognizing Your Unique Abilities and Purpose: In Philippians 2:13, the word of God says, *"For it is God which worketh in you both to will and to do of his good pleasure."* Hence, acknowledge the distinct gifts and talents God has endowed you with.

Surrendering to God's Will: Submit your plans and desires to God, trusting that His plans for you are good. *"For I know the thoughts that I think toward you, saith the* LORD, *thoughts of peace, and not of evil, to give you an expected end"* (Jeremiah 29:11).

Striving to Fulfill His Plans: Actively pursue the path God has set before you, relying on His strength and guidance.

Philippians 4:13 reminds us, *"I can do all things through Christ who strengthens me."* This verse underscores that with God, you can achieve far more than you could on your own.

In essence, trusting in God's providence, stepping out in faith and aligning our lives with His will are essential components of unlocking and manifesting our God-given potential. Through prayer, obedience and a steadfast commitment to following Christ, we can walk boldly in the path He has set before us, fulfilling His purposes and bringing glory to His name.

Understanding and maximizing one's potential is a sacred responsibility bestowed by God. By aligning our lives with His purpose, embracing His gifts and continually seeking His guidance, we unlock the fullness of our God-given potential, glorifying Him through our growth, achievements and contributions to His Kingdom.

4

Leveraging Your Unique Talents and Abilities

In His boundless wisdom and creativity, God has endowed everyone with a distinct array of talents and abilities. These gifts, intricately woven into the very fabric of our being, are not random occurrences, but purposefully crafted to fulfill His divine plan for our lives. As believers, it is crucial that we grasp and embrace these God-given talents, understanding them as tools through which we can glorify Him and serve others. The Bible underscores the concept of individual uniqueness and giftedness.

In 1 Corinthians 12, the apostle Paul employs the analogy of the human body to illustrate the diversity of spiritual gifts within the church. Just as the body consists of various parts with distinct functions, believers are enriched with diverse gifts by the Holy Spirit. Each gift plays a vital role in the edification and unity of the body of Christ (1 Corinthians 12:4-11).

Additionally, in Romans 12:6-8, Paul encourages believers to utilize their gifts in accordance with the grace bestowed upon them, whether it be prophecy, service, teaching, exhortation, giving, leadership or mercy. These gifts are not for personal gain, but for the collective benefit of the body and the advancement of God's Kingdom.

Psalms 139:14 reminds us that we are fearfully and wonderfully made by God, each possessing unique qualities and strengths that reflect His divine craftsmanship. Furthermore, Ephesians 2:10 teaches us that we are God's masterpiece, created in Christ Jesus to carry out good works prepared in advance for us. Therefore, acknowledging and employing our strengths aligns with God's purpose for our lives.

In the journey of life, however, embracing our unique talents and strengths is not only a personal endeavour, but also a spiritual calling. As believers, we are called to recognize and celebrate the individual gifts that God has bestowed upon us, knowing that they are essential components of His divine plan for our lives.

Bible affirms the importance of recognizing and utilizing our God-given talents and strengths. In 1 Corinthians 12, Paul compares the body of Christ to a physical body, highlighting the diversity of gifts within the church. Just as each part of the body has a unique function, so too do believers possess distinct talents and strengths given by the Holy Spirit. These gifts are meant to be used for the common good and the glory of God (1 Corinthians 12:4-7).

Additionally, in Colossians 3:23-24, we are reminded that whatever we do, we are to do it with all our heart, as working for the Lord rather than for human masters. This includes utilizing our talents and strengths in our daily endeavours, whether it be in our careers, relationships or service to others. Therefore, begin today by seeking God's guidance through prayer and introspection. Reflect on your past experiences, accomplishments and areas where you feel most fulfilled. Ask the Holy Spirit to reveal your unique talents and strengths in accordance with God's will.

Take time to identify your talents and strengths by reflecting on what brings you joy, what comes naturally to you and what aligns with your core values and beliefs. Consider the skills and qualities you have demonstrated in past successes and achievements. Once you have identified your talents and strengths, seek ways to integrate them into your daily life.

Look for opportunities that align with your interests and passions, whether it be in your career, hobbies or community involvement. Surround yourself with mentors, collaborators and fellow believers who can support you in honing your talents and strengths. Seek out individuals who appreciate and value your unique gifts and who can provide guidance and encouragement along the way.

Embracing your unique talents and strengths often involves stepping outside of your comfort zone and taking on new challenges. Embrace these opportunities for growth, knowing that failure is a natural part of the learning process. Every experience, successful or not, is an opportunity for spiritual growth and development. Trust in God's plan for your life and His provision for your unique talents and strengths. Surrender your talents to Him, knowing that He will use them for His glory and the good of others.

Again, the infinite God has created everyone uniquely with inherent abilities and talents. Psalms

139:14 affirms this truth, stating, *"I will praise thee; for I am fearfully and wonderfully made: marvellous are thy works; and that my soul knoweth right well."* From this verse, we recognize that God intricately designed each person with specific gifts and qualities.

Moreover, in Romans 12:6-8, the apostle Paul discusses spiritual gifts within the body of Christ, emphasizing the importance of recognizing and utilizing these gifts for the benefit of the church. This passage highlights the diversity of talents and abilities among believers, indicating that each person has something valuable to contribute. Therefore, it is essential for individuals to take the time to uncover and acknowledge their unique abilities. Just as the parable of the talents in Matthew 25:14-30 teaches us, we are called to invest and develop the gifts that God has entrusted to us. By doing so, we not only honour God's design, but also fulfill our purpose in His Kingdom.

Embracing our unique talents is not about pride or self-glorification, but about stewardship and service. As mentioned in 1 Peter 4:10-11, *"As every man hath received the gift, even so minister the same one to another, as good stewards of the manifold grace of God. If any man speak, let him speak as the oracles of God; if any man minister, let him do it as of the ability which God giveth: that God in all things may be glorified through Jesus Christ, to whom be praise and dominion for ever and ever. Amen."*

A Recap

Recognize Your Gifts: In Romans 12:6-8, Paul writes, *"Having then gifts differing according to the grace that is given to us, whether prophecy, let us prophesy according to* *the proportion of faith; Or ministry, let us wait on our ministering: or he that teacheth, on teaching; Or he that exhorteth, on exhortation: he that giveth, let him do it with simplicity; he that ruleth, with diligence; he that sheweth mercy, with cheerfulness."* This passage encourages us to recognize and use our unique gifts. God has endowed each of us with specific abilities and we are called to use them for His glory and the benefit of others.

Use Your Talents for Good: In the Parable of the Talents (Matthew 25:14-30), Jesus teaches about the importance of using our talents and abilities for good. The servants who use their talents wisely are rewarded, while the servant who hides his talent out of fear is reprimanded. This parable emphasizes the responsibility we have to actively invest our talents in ways that produce spiritual and practical fruit.

Trust in God's Plan: Jeremiah 29:11 says, *"For I know the thoughts that I think toward you, saith the LORD, thoughts of peace, and not of evil, to give you an expected end."* This verse reassures us that God has a unique plan for each of us and we should trust in His plan as we use our talents and abilities. God's plans are designed for our ultimate good and His glory and trusting Him allows us to navigate life with confidence and hope.

Work Diligently: Colossians 3:23-24 states, *"And whatsoever ye do, do it heartily, as to the Lord, and not unto men; Knowing that of the Lord ye shall receive the reward of the inheritance: for ye serve the Lord Christ."* This encourages us to work diligently and use our talents to serve God. Our efforts should be wholehearted, reflecting our dedication to Christ and our desire to honour Him in all we do.

Therefore, whether it be painting, writing, problem-solving or any other talent, we should recognize these abilities as gifts from God and seek to use them for His glory. By embracing our unique talents and developing them to their fullest potential, we can shine brightly as reflections of God's creativity and goodness in the world. Through these, your unique talents and strengths in alignment with biblical principles, you can live a more authentic, fulfilling life and make a positive impact on the world around you. Trust in God's guidance, take bold steps of faith and celebrate the unique gifts He has entrusted to you.

5

Overcoming Limiting Beliefs and Self-Doubt

We understand that our beliefs and perceptions are shaped by various influences throughout our lives. Proverbs 23:7 states, *"For as he thinketh in his heart, so is he: Eat and drink, saith he to thee; but his heart is not with thee."* This verse emphasizes the power of our thoughts and beliefs in shaping our identity and actions.

Limiting beliefs are deeply ingrained convictions or assumptions that often stem from early life experiences, societal norms or past failures. These beliefs act as filters through which we interpret events and make decisions, influencing our confidence and motivation.

One source of limiting beliefs is childhood experiences. Negative feedback or criticism during childhood can create self-doubt and limit our potential. Proverbs 22:6 advises, *"Train up a child in the way he should go: and when he is old, he will not depart from it."* This highlights the importance of positive reinforcement and encouragement during formative years.

Societal conditioning also plays a significant role in shaping our beliefs. Society imposes expectations and norms that can restrict our choices and create self-imposed boundaries. Romans 12:2 urges us not to conform to the patterns of this world, but to be transformed by the renewing of our minds, emphasizing the need to align our beliefs with God's truth rather than societal standards.

Past failures can also contribute to limiting beliefs, instilling fear and self-doubt. However, Philippians 3:13-14 encourages us to forget what is behind and press on toward the goal, reminding us that our past does not define our future. Through faith in God's grace and redemption, we can overcome past failures and move forward with confidence.

Furthermore, comparisons and negative influences, including social media and unsupportive relationships, can reinforce limiting beliefs and decrease self-esteem. Proverbs 13:20 warns, *"He that walketh with wise men shall be wise: but a companion of fools shall be destroyed."*

Surrounding ourselves with positive influences and seeking wisdom from God's Word can help counteract these negative influences and strengthen our faith in our abilities.

Limiting beliefs may stem from various sources, we have the power to overcome them through faith, positive reinforcement and aligning our beliefs with God's truth. By renewing our minds and seeking wisdom from Scripture, we can break free from the grip of limiting beliefs and live according to God's purpose for our lives.

Proverbs 4:23 advises, *"Keep thy heart with all diligence; for out of it are the issues of life."*

This verse emphasizes the significance of maintaining a positive mindset and overcoming obstacles that hinder our spiritual and personal development.

Limiting beliefs can hinder various aspects of our lives, including career advancement, personal relationships and overall well-being. They act as self-imposed barriers that prevent us from reaching our full potential and experiencing the abundant life that God desires for us.

Understanding and addressing beliefs that limit us is crucial for personal growth and spiritual development. These beliefs often stem from a distorted perception of us which contradicts the truth of God's Word. Let's delve deeper into how we can overcome these limiting beliefs:

Recognize the Source: When examining beliefs that limit us, it's essential to identify their root cause. Often, we are our own worst critics, negative views of ourselves that are contrary to God's perspective. Ephesians 1:6 reminds us that we are accepted in the Beloved, emphasizing our worth in Christ. Like others, who struggled with low self-worth, we may internalize negative feedback from others, leading to self-doubt and diminished confidence.

Combat Lies with Truth: Jesus demonstrated the power of God's Word in overcoming doubt and temptation. We, too, can use Scripture to challenge and break free from the lies we believe about ourselves. Hebrews 4:12 affirms that *"the word of God is quick, and powerful, and sharper than any twoedged sword, piercing even to the dividing asunder of soul and spirit, and of the joints and marrow, and is a discerner of the thoughts and intents of the heart."*

The word is capable of exposing the lies and falsehoods that hinder our faith. By aligning our thoughts with God's truth, we can dismantle the strongholds of doubt and unbelief in our lives

Embrace God's Design: Despite our struggles with limiting beliefs, we must remember that our potential is God-given and He has designed us for a specific purpose.

Jeremiah 29:11 assures us that God has plans for our welfare and not for evil, to give us a future and a hope. However, insecurity, guilt, shame and fear often cloud our perception of God's purpose for our lives, hindering us from stepping into our divine calling.

Renew Your Mind: Transforming our minds is essential for overcoming limiting beliefs and aligning ourselves with God's will. Romans 12:2 urges us not to be conformed to the patterns of this world, but to be transformed by the renewing of our minds. This process involves replacing negative thought patterns with God's truth, allowing His Word to shape our identity and perspective.

Unlock Your Potential: Limiting beliefs prevent us from exploring our true potential and discovering our talents and abilities. Jeremiah 29:11 assures us that God has plans to prosper us and give us hope for the future. By overcoming these beliefs, we open ourselves to new opportunities and personal growth, aligning ourselves with God's purpose for our lives.

Increase Self-confidence: Limiting beliefs erode our self-confidence and self-esteem, leading to feelings of inadequacy and doubt. However, Psalms 139:14 reminds us that we are fearfully and wonderfully made by God.

By overcoming these beliefs, we build resilience, belief in oneself and empowerment, trusting in God's strength and guidance.

Expand Your Comfort Zone: Limiting beliefs create a comfort zone that keeps us within familiar boundaries, preventing us from stepping out in faith and embracing new challenges. However, Joshua 1:9 encourages us to be strong and courageous, not to be afraid or discouraged, for the Lord our God is with us wherever we go. By challenging and overcoming these beliefs, we can expand our comfort zone and grow in faith, embracing new experiences and opportunities.

Achieve Success: Limiting beliefs act as roadblocks on the path to success, hindering us from pursuing our goals and dreams. However, Philippians 4:13 reminds us that we can do all things through Christ Who strengthens us. By breaking free from these self-imposed limitations, we can pursue our goals with renewed determination and succeed, trusting in God's provision and guidance.

Improve Relationships: Poor relationship can hinder healthy relationships by creating barriers to intimacy, trust and vulnerability. However, Ephesians 4:32 encourages us to be kind and compassionate to one another, forgiving each other, just as in Christ God forgave us. By overcoming these weaknesses, we can foster deeper connections and more fulfilling relationships, reflecting God's love and grace to others.

Overcoming limiting beliefs is crucial for personal growth, success and spiritual maturity. By aligning our thoughts and beliefs with God's truth, we can break free from self-imposed barriers and live a life of purpose, fulfillment and joy. Hence, we can break free from the chains of self-doubt and insecurity, stepping boldly into the abundant life God has promised us.

6

Seeking God's Guidance and Direction

When faced with the dilemma of choosing the lesser of two evils, it is imperative to anchor our decision-making in the strong biblical teaching that emphasizes seeking God's will above all else. Despite the fact that God is sovereign over all things, He does not direct us to choose between options that contradict His revealed will. In such moments, rather than settling for the lesser of two evils, we should surrender our decision to the pursuit of a life that reflects holiness, righteousness and obedience to His Word.

Mysticism, although appealing in its promise of direct spiritual knowledge, falls short of the truth encapsulated in Scripture. It suggests that personal encounters or subjective experiences can supplant the authority of God's Word. However, such beliefs lead us astray, as they bypass the essence of God's revealed will. Historical examples, like Ignatius of Loyola's visions, underscore the dangers of relying on mystical experiences divorced from Scriptural truths which can lead to actions contrary to God's Word.

In addition, seeking signs or tests to confirm what we already know can detract from the clarity of God's guidance. While God may, at times, accommodate our weaknesses by providing signs, Scripture already furnishes us with His will on many matters. Demanding continuous proofs undermines the trust and faithfulness inherent in God's Word, akin to Gideon's fleece or Moses' request for signs.

In our pursuit of God's will, we must avoid falling into these pitfalls. They divert us from the path of genuine discernment and obedience. Instead, we should remain steadfast in anchoring our decisions in Scripture, trusting in its timeless wisdom to guide our steps and illuminate our way forward.

When life seems chaotic and nothing goes as planned, it is crucial to lean on the strong biblical teaching that underscores the importance of trusting in God's sovereign plan. Despite the storms we face, we are called to trust that God will always pave a way where there seems to be none. His love for us is unfailing and His plans for our lives are intricately woven with purpose and intentionality. Even when it feels like the burdens, we carry are overwhelming, we can take solace in knowing that God never burdens us beyond what we can bear.

In those moments, it is an opportunity to evaluate our faith and deepen our trust in Him. Though the challenges may seem daunting, God's plan remains steadfast, guiding us toward growth and strength. *"And thine ears shall hear a word behind thee, saying, this is the way, walk ye in it, when ye turn to the right hand, and when ye turn to the left"* (Isaiah 30:21).

Prayer becomes our refuge in times of uncertainty as we seek God's guidance on how to navigate the complexities of life according to His divine will.

Ecclesiastes 3:1 reminds us that there is a time for everything, even in the darkest moments, God is at work, molding us according to His purpose. Scripture teaches us that God's plan, often referred to as His will, is centered on glorifying Him in all that we do.

Romans 12:1-2 exhorts us to present ourselves as living sacrifices, wholly devoted to God's service. By renewing our minds and aligning our actions with His will, we can discern what is good, acceptable and perfect in His sight. In essence, when life feels overwhelming and directionless, we can find assurance in God's plan for our lives. Through trust, prayer and obedience to His will, we can navigate challenges with confidence, knowing that God is using every circumstance to shape us into vessels of His purpose and strength.

The concept of God's sovereign will encompass His control over all aspects of existence, spanning across time, space and the visible as well as the invisible realms. Despite this sovereignty, humanity retains the gift of free will, granting us the ability to discern between right and wrong. It's crucial to recognize that while God permits actions that go against His nature, His ultimate plan remains sovereign and just.

Amid life's challenges, 1 Peter 3:17-18 reminds us that suffering for doing good aligns with God's will. Even Christ Himself suffered unjustly, bearing the weight of humanity's sins to reconcile us with God. This underscores the redemptive power of suffering and the alignment of our will with God's divine purpose, even in the face of adversity.

The Bible serves as a beacon of light, illuminating the paths we tread and offering wisdom for living in accordance with God's will. Through Scripture, we uncover insights into our spiritual gifts and strengths, discerning our purpose in life. By cultivating a personal relationship with God through prayer, fasting and fellowship, we deepen our understanding of His plan and purpose for our lives.

The journey may be marked by trials and uncertainties, but trusting in God's plan requires unwavering obedience and faith. Even when circumstances seem dire, we are called to align our choices with God's truth, knowing that His guidance will lead us on the path of righteousness. Though we may not comprehend every aspect of His plan, surrendering to His will brings ultimate fulfillment and peace. With trust in God's guiding hand, we can rest assured that He will provide for our needs and lead us to fulfill His purpose for our lives on earth.

In Seeking God's Guidance, Ask for Guidance: James 1:5 tells us, *"If any of you lack wisdom, let him ask of God, that giveth to all men liberally, and upbraideth not; and it shall be given him."* This verse encourages us to actively seek God's guidance and assures us that He is willing to provide it. When we feel uncertain or lack wisdom, turning to God in prayer and asking for His guidance is essential. God's generosity in providing wisdom is a testament to His loving nature and His desire for us to make wise decisions.

Trust in the Lord: Proverbs 3:5-6 says, *"Trust in the LORD with all thine heart; and lean not unto thine own understanding. In all thy ways acknowledge him, and he shall direct thy paths."* This passage emphasizes the importance of trusting in God's wisdom over our own and submitting our plans to Him. Trusting God means having confidence in His ability to guide us, even when we do not understand the path ahead. By submitting to His will, we acknowledge that His plans are superior to ours and that He will lead us in the right direction.

Seek God's Will: In Matthew 6:10, Jesus teaches us to pray, *"Thy kingdom come, Thy will be done in earth, as it is in heaven."* This is a reminder to seek God's will in all things, as His plans are perfect and good. Seeking God's will involves aligning our desires and actions with His purposes. When we pray for God's will to be done, we surrender our own agendas and invite His divine plan to unfold in our lives, trusting that it is for our ultimate good.

Listen to the Holy Spirit: John 14:26 says, *"But the Comforter, which is the Holy Ghost, whom the Father will send in my name, he shall teach you all things, and bring all things to your remembrance, whatsoever I have said unto you."* This verse reminds us that the Holy Spirit is our Guide and Teacher, helping us to understand God's direction for our lives. The Holy Spirit plays a crucial role in revealing God's truths to us and guiding us in our daily decisions. By being attentive to the Holy Spirit's promptings, we can gain clarity and insight into God's will.

Wait Patiently: Psalms 27:14 advises, *"Wait on the LORD: be of good courage, and he shall strengthen thine heart: wait, I say, on the LORD."* Sometimes, seeking God's guidance means waiting patiently for His timing. Patience is an important virtue in the process of seeking divine direction. God's timing is perfect and waiting on Him strengthens our faith and trust. While we wait, we can take heart, knowing that God's plans for us are unfolding in His perfect time.

Therefore, aligning our desires with God's will and trusting that He knows what is best for us is the essence of seeking divine guidance. As we actively seek His direction, we can have confidence in His unfailing love and perfect plan for our lives. God's guidance is always worth waiting for and His direction is always best. Remember, His wisdom surpasses ours and His plans for us are designed for our ultimate good and His glory.

7

Discovering Your Passion and Purpose

Understanding and utilizing our unique personal qualities and gifts is a journey intertwined with spiritual principles found in biblical principles. Central to this journey is the pursuit of passion, a deep-seated enthusiasm that ignites our souls and drives us toward purposeful action. Have you ever experienced the sensation of merely going through the motions in life, lacking a clear sense of direction or fulfillment? Do you find yourself pondering your true calling, unsure of how to best utilize your time and talents? If these questions resonate with you, rest assured, you are not alone.

Many individuals grapple with the quest to discover their passion and purpose, particularly in a world teeming with options and distractions. However, uncovering your passion and purpose is not an insurmountable task; rather, it can be a deeply rewarding and meaningful journey. Passion and purpose, though intertwined, each holds distinct significance in shaping an authentic and fulfilling life. Passion is that which ignites your spirit, infusing you with energy and enthusiasm, while purpose provides a sense of direction, meaning and contribution to the world.

In discerning our passions, we can draw wisdom from Scriptures on the nature of our desires and inclinations. Psalms 37:4 urges us to delight ourselves in the Lord, trusting that He will grant us the desires of our hearts. This suggests that our passions are intricately connected to our relationship with God, aligning with His purposes for our lives.

Identifying our passions involves introspection and self-awareness, recognizing the activities that stir our souls and energize our spirits. Romans 12:6-8 speaks about the diversity of gifts bestowed upon believers by the Holy Spirit, emphasizing the importance of recognizing and utilizing these gifts in service to others. Similarly, 1 Corinthians 12:4-7 highlights the varied manifestations of spiritual gifts, indicating that our passions may be closely tied to these God-given abilities.

Moreover, the pursuit of passion necessitates humility as we acknowledge that our talents and abilities are gifts from God. Philippians 2:3-4 encourages us to consider others as more significant than ourselves, emphasizing a selfless attitude in the exploration of our passions. By leaving our egos at the door, we open ourselves to divine guidance and revelation regarding our true passions and purposes.

When passion and purpose converge, they form a formidable catalyst propelling you toward your aspirations, empowering you to surmount obstacles and effect positive change; but how does one discern their passion and purpose in life? Here are some biblical-inspired insights to guide your journey:

Cultivate curiosity, attentiveness and openness to new experiences. Scripture encourages us to seek wisdom and understanding (Proverbs 2:2-5), urging us to explore diverse interests, activities and causes. By remaining curious about the world and receptive to new opportunities, you may uncover passions and purposes previously unknown.

Identify needs and causes that resonate with your heart. Galatians 6:2 implores us to bear one another's burdens, emphasizing the importance of empathy and service. Pay heed to issues that stir compassion within you, discerning how you can contribute to solutions and make a positive impact in the lives of others.

Reflect on your childhood for inspiration. Jesus extols the innocence and authenticity of children, urging us to emulate their faith and humility (Matthew 18:3-4). Recall the activities and aspirations of your youth, as they may offer insights into your inherent passions and purposes, unencumbered by societal expectations or limitations.

Recognize and pursue activities that immerse you so deeply that time seems to slip away. Passion often manifests when you enter a state of flow, fully engrossed and enjoying the task at hand. In these moments, work feels effortless and joy permeates your efforts. Take note of the activities that captivate you in this way and make a concerted effort to engage in them more frequently. By nurturing these pursuits, you may discover profound fulfillment and joy as you leverage your strengths and talents.

Begin with small steps and keep the journey enjoyable. Discovering your passion and purpose need not be an overwhelming endeavour. You can initiate the process by dedicating a few minutes each day to activities that bring you happiness. Experiment with various hobbies or projects that spark your interest, allowing yourself the freedom to explore without pressure. Consider social groups or communities aligned with your passions to further enrich your experiences. Embrace the process with a light-hearted attitude, relishing the adventure of uncovering what ignites your spirit.

Safeguard your newfound passions and purpose by prioritizing them in your life. Once identified, these pursuits deserve your unwavering commitment and protection from distractions. Establish clear goals and action plans to consistently and effectively pursue your passions. Allocate dedicated time in your schedule and set boundaries to preserve your focus. Refrain from activities that detract from your purpose or drain your energy, surrounding yourself instead with individuals who champion your journey and inspire growth.

Determine how to leverage your passions and skills to achieve your unique objectives and address your individual challenges. Discovering your passion and purpose is merely the first step; the next is to translate these insights into tangible actions that create value and impact. This may involve introspection, experimentation and seeking guidance to identify your niche and direction.

Remain open to refining your approach through research, feedback and continued exploration. *"So that thou incline thine ear unto wisdom, and apply thine heart to understanding; Yea, if thou criest after knowledge, and liftest up thy voice for understanding; If thou seekest her as silver, and searchest for her as for hid treasures; Then shalt thou understand the fear of the LORD and find the knowledge of God "*(Proverbs 2:2-5).

In navigating the journey of discovering your passion and purpose, draw strength from the wisdom of Scripture and the guidance of the Holy Spirit. By embracing curiosity, empathy and introspection, you can unveil the unique gifts and calling that God has bestowed upon you, enriching your life with purpose and fulfillment. Through prayer, reflection and discernment, we can uncover the passions that fuel our souls and contribute to the flourishing of God's purpose on earth.

8

Developing a Growth Mindset

The principles of a growth mindset resonate with biblical teachings on perseverance, humility and reliance on God's grace. By integrating these principles into our lives, we can cultivate a mindset that fosters continuous learning, resilience and personal development, ultimately glorifying God in all that we do. Scripture emphasizes the importance of maintaining a healthy mindset, both on and off the proverbial "golf course" of life.

The power of our thoughts and the importance of cultivating a mindset for growth is deeply rooted in the Holy Scripture. *"Finally, brethren, whatsoever things are true, whatsoever things are honest, whatsoever things are just, whatsoever things are pure, whatsoever things are lovely, whatsoever things are of good report; if there be any virtue, and if there be any praise, think on these things."*

This Philippians 4:8 instructs believers to focus their minds on whatever is true, noble, right, pure, lovely and admirable, emphasizing the transformative impact of meditation on godly principles. In addition, *"Meditate upon these things; give thyself wholly to them; that thy profiting may appear to all."* This 1 Timothy 4:15

encourages individuals to meditate on and fully devote themselves to spiritual teachings, recognizing that such dedication leads to evident progress in one's life.

The connection between our internal thoughts and external reality finds resonance in biblical principles as well. Proverbs 23:7a declares that, *"For as he thinketh in his heart, so is he,"* highlighting the profound influence of our thoughts on shaping our identity and actions.

Moreover, Romans 12:2 urges believers not to conform to the pattern of this world, but to be transformed by the renewing of their minds, underscoring the importance of aligning our thoughts with God's truth to experience lasting transformation.

Scripture also affirms the inherent greatness of everyone, bestowed with unique talents and abilities by their Creator. Psalms 139:14 celebrates the truth that each person is fearfully and wonderfully made, reflecting God's divine craftsmanship.

Ephesians 2:10 further emphasizes that believers are God's handiwork, created in Christ Jesus to do good works prepared in advance for them to do, affirming the intrinsic value and purpose imbued within every individual.

Our responsibility, therefore, is to steward the gifts and talents entrusted to us by God, maximizing them for His glory and the betterment of humanity. This aligns with the biblical concept of stewardship, where believers are called to faithfully manage and develop the resources entrusted to them by God (Matthew 25:14-30).

Cultivating a mindset for growth, as advocated in the biblical framework, involves embracing a posture of continuous learning, improvement and reliance on

God's guidance. It requires surrendering our thoughts and aspirations to God's will, trusting in His plans for our lives and allowing His transformative power to work within us.

Moreover, the biblical concept of stewardship applies not only to personal talents and resources, but also to organizational culture and practices. Ephesians 4:29 admonishes believers to speak only what is helpful for building others up, emphasizing the importance of fostering an environment of respect, encouragement and constructive communication.

In a professional setting, cultivating a growth mindset involves creating a culture that values openness, innovation and continuous improvement. This aligns with biblical principles of humility, teamwork and accountability.

Proverbs 15:22 teaches that plans fail for lack of counsel, but with many advisers, they succeed, highlighting the importance of seeking diverse perspectives and feedback within organizations.

Leadership modelled after the servant-hearted example of Jesus Christ fosters an environment where individuals feel empowered to share their thoughts and ideas without fear of retribution. Philippians 2:3-4 urges believers to consider others above themselves, modelling humility and empathy in leadership.

Organizations that prioritize a growth mindset experience greater innovation, collaboration and resilience. By creating an environment where individuals feel valued, respected and rewarded for their contributions, organizations can tap into the full potential of their workforce and fulfill their mission with excellence. As we meditate on His word, devote ourselves to His teachings and steward our gifts for His glory, we experience the abundant life He promises and become agents of positive change in the world.

The biblical narrative is replete with examples of individuals who demonstrated a growth mindset in their pursuit of excellence and fulfillment of their God-given purposes.

Consider the story of David, who, through faith and perseverance, rose from a shepherd boy to become a mighty king or the apostle Paul, who continuously sought to grow in his understanding and application of God's truth despite facing numerous challenges and setbacks.

In aligning with biblical principles, here are some ways to develop a growth mindset:

Identify Your Mindset: Reflect on your approach to challenges and opportunities, recognizing whether your mindset leans more toward fixed or growth-oriented thinking. Proverbs 4:23 encourages believers to guard their hearts, for from them flow the springs of life, emphasizing the importance of self-awareness in shaping our perspectives.

Acknowledge Your Improvements: Reflect on areas in which you have experienced growth and improvement over time, recognizing the role of effort and perseverance in your progress. Philippians 1:6 assures believers that God Who began a good work in them will carry it on to completion until the day of Christ Jesus, underscoring the ongoing nature of spiritual and personal growth.

Learn from Others' Success: Study the achievements of others, particularly those who have overcome adversity or defied the odds. Hebrews 12:1 encourages believers to run with perseverance the race marked out for them, looking to Jesus as the ultimate example of endurance and triumph.

Seek Feedback: Humbly seek feedback from others, recognizing the value of constructive criticism in your journey toward growth and improvement. Proverbs 15:31 teaches that heeding constructive criticism leads to wisdom and understanding, highlighting the importance of humility in receiving feedback.

Harness the Power of 'Yet': The concept of 'yet' reflects the biblical principle of hope and perseverance. Romans 5:3-4 encourages believers to rejoice in their sufferings, knowing that suffering produces perseverance, character and hope. Similarly, the idea that one may not be skilled in certain areas 'yet' acknowledges the potential for growth and improvement through diligent effort and reliance on God's grace.

Learn Something New: Proverbs 18:15 reminds us that an intelligent heart acquires knowledge and the ear of the wise seeks knowledge. Learning new skills and stepping out of our comfort zones align with the biblical call to pursue wisdom and understanding. By embracing new challenges, we demonstrate faith in God's ability to equip us for every good work (2 Timothy 3:17).

Learn From Your Mistakes: Ecclesiastes 7:20 teaches that *"for there is not a just man upon earth, that doeth good, and sinneth not,"* highlighting the inevitability of human error. Rather than viewing mistakes as failures, we can approach them as opportunities for growth and refinement.

"*For a just man falleth seven times, and riseth up again: but the wicked shall fall into mischief.*" This verse in Proverbs 24:16 encourages us not to give up in times of adversity, but to rise again, recognizing that resilience and perseverance lead to maturity and wisdom.

Be Kind to Yourself: Ephesians 4:32 instructs believers "*And be ye kind one to another, tender-hearted, forgiving one another, even as God for Christ's sake hath forgiven you.*" Extending grace and compassion to ourselves aligns with this biblical principle, fostering a mindset of self-compassion and resilience. By treating ourselves with kindness, we create space for growth and transformation to occur.

Look at Examples: Hebrews 12:1-2 encourages believers to fix their eyes on Jesus, the Pioneer and Perfecter of our faith, drawing inspiration from His example of endurance and perseverance. Similarly, studying the lives of those who embody a growth mindset can provide valuable insights and encouragement for our own journey of growth and development.

Set Realistic Goals: Proverbs 16:9 reminds us that "*a man's heart deviseth his way: but the LORD directeth his steps.*" Setting realistic goals aligned with God's purposes allows us to exercise faith and stewardship while remaining open to His guidance and direction.

By committing our plans to the Lord, we trust in His provision and timing for our growth and success.

By integrating these practices into our lives, we can cultivate a growth mindset that aligns with biblical principles of diligent effort, wise counsel and reliance on God's guidance which will empower us to fulfill our potential and glorify God in all that we do.

9

Setting Clear and Meaningful Goals

Goal setting is the process of identifying specific objectives or targets that an individual or organization wants to achieve. It involves determining what needs to be accomplished, setting measurable and realistic goals and creating a plan to reach those goals. Goal setting helps to provide direction, motivation and focus; and allows for progress to be tracked and evaluated. It is an important tool for personal development, professional growth and organizational success. Goal setting emphasizes the importance of aligning our aspirations with God's will and purpose for our lives, with Christ serving as the ultimate Role Model for setting and pursuing meaningful objectives.

Scripture affirms the value of setting goals that reflect and enhance our God-given selves. Philippians 3:14 encourages believers to press on toward the goal for the prize of the upward call of God in Christ Jesus, highlighting the pursuit of spiritual growth and fulfillment in Christ as the overall objective. As we seek to emulate Christ's example and fulfill our God-given potential, setting goals becomes a means of honouring God and serving others.

Moreover, secular research corroborates the effectiveness of goal setting in enhancing performance and productivity. However, biblical wisdom reminds us that our goals should not be driven solely by personal ambition or worldly success. Proverbs 16:3 exhorts believers to commit their plans to the Lord, knowing that He will establish their steps. Our goals must be aligned with God's will, reflecting His purposes and bringing glory to His name.

The brevity and uncertainty of life underscore the need for humility and dependence on God in the goal-setting process. James 4:14 reminds us of the fleeting nature of life, urging us to submit our plans to God's sovereign will. Rather than presuming on the future, we acknowledge God's sovereignty and trust Him to guide and direct our steps according to His purposes.

The biblical example of Moses in Exodus 9:16 illustrates the importance of aligning our goals with God's overarching plan for His glory and the advancement of His Kingdom. As God raised up Moses to demonstrate His power and declare His name to all the earth, so too should our goals be oriented toward magnifying God's greatness and proclaiming His glory in all that we do.

Applying these biblical principles in your goal-setting process can lead to successful advancement in your career. By setting goals that are in line with your values and priorities, you can effectively manage your tasks, meet deadlines and pursue achievable aims. Here are seven tips rooted in sound biblical teaching to consider when setting goals:

Set SMART goals: Adopt the SMART method, a framework deeply rooted in biblical wisdom. This approach ensures that your goals are Specific, Measurable, Attainable, Relevant and Time-bound. Specific goals are clearly defined and purposeful, measurable goals allow you to track progress, attainable goals are realistic and within your capabilities, relevant goals align with your values and passions and time-bound goals provide a sense of urgency and focus.

Write your goals: Scripture encourages the practice of writing down goals as a means of commitment and accountability. Habakkuk 2:2 harps, *"And the LORD answered me, and said, Write the vision, and make it plain upon tables, that he may run that readeth it."* By documenting your goals in a journal or digital format, you take ownership of your objectives and create a tangible record to reference and reflect upon. When crafting your goals, use positive language and affirmations, expressing certainty and determination in achieving them.

Prioritize prayer and seek divine guidance: Involve God in your goal-setting process by seeking His wisdom and direction. Proverbs 3:5-6 advises, *"Trust in the LORD with all thine heart; and lean not unto thine own understanding. In all thy ways acknowledge him, and he shall direct thy paths."* Prayerful consideration ensures that your goals align with God's will for your life and enables you to surrender your plans to His sovereign guidance.

Cultivate perseverance and resilience: Embrace the biblical virtues of perseverance and resilience as you pursue your goals. James 1:12 assures, *"Blessed is the man that endureth temptation (or who perseveres under trial): for* *when he is tried, he shall receive the crown of life, which the Lord hath promised to them that love him."* Expect challenges and setbacks along the way, but remain steadfast in your faith and determination to overcome obstacles and achieve your objectives.

Foster accountability and community support: Engage in accountability partnerships and seek support from fellow believers to uphold your commitment to your goals. Ecclesiastes 4:9-10 emphasizes the strength found in community, stating, *"Two are better than one, because they have a good reward for their labour. For if they fall, the one will lift up his fellow: but woe to him that is alone when he falleth; for he hath not another to help him up."* Sharing your poster with trusted individuals fosters encouragement, accountability and mutual growth.

Reflect and adjust as needed: Regularly assess your progress and adjust your goals as necessary, remaining open to divine redirection and refinement. Proverbs 20:5 advises, *"Counsel in the heart of man is like deep water; but a man of understanding will draw it out."* Reflect on your goals in light of God's guidance and discernment, making any modifications needed to stay aligned with His purposes and priorities.

Develop an action plan: Scripture encourages diligent planning and preparation as a means of stewarding our resources and maximizing our effectiveness in achieving goals. Proverbs 21:5 teaches, *"The thoughts of the diligent tend only to plenteousness; but of every one that is hasty only to want."* By developing an action plan rooted in biblical wisdom, you can effectively translate your goals into tangible steps for accomplishment. Here are steps to create an action plan with spiritual application:

Define the goal: Begin by prayerfully discerning your goal and crafting a goal statement that aligns with God's purposes for your life. Ensure that your goal is Specific, Measurable, Attainable, Relevant and Time-bound (SMART), reflecting your commitment to honouring God in your pursuits.

Identify essential tasks: Seek divine guidance to discern the necessary actions required to achieve your goal.

Prioritize these tasks according to their importance and establish deadlines for completion, trusting in God's provision and guidance.

Analyze each task: Consider the resources, time, and potential challenges associated with each task, relying on God's strength and wisdom to overcome obstacles.

Adapt your plan as needed to reflect changing circumstances, remaining flexible and receptive to divine redirection.

Adjust the plan: Continuously evaluate and adjust your action plan in light of God's leading and your evolving circumstances. Surrender your plans to God's sovereign will, trusting that He will direct your steps and bring about His purposes in His perfect timing.

Consider your strengths and weaknesses: Scripture teaches that God has uniquely gifted each individual for His purposes and glory. Romans 12:6 affirms, *"Having then gifts differing according to the grace that is given to us, whether prophecy, let us prophesy according to the proportion of faith."*

By prayerfully assessing your strengths and weaknesses, you can align your goals with your God-given abilities and discern the most effective strategies for success. Acknowledge your dependence on God's strength in areas of weakness, trusting that His power is made perfect in your weakness (2 Corinthians 12:9).

Focus on one goal at a time: James 1:8 cautions against being double-minded, reminding believers that a double-minded person is unstable in all their ways. Rather than spreading yourself thin by pursuing multiple goals simultaneously, prioritize one major goal at a time.

By focusing your energy and attention on a single objective, you can devote your full effort to its accomplishment, trusting in God's guidance and provision along the way. Remain steadfast in your commitment to honouring God through diligent pursuit of His purposes, knowing that He will grant wisdom and strength to navigate the journey.

Aligning Your Goals with Divine Purpose: In the journey of life, it is essential to regularly review and update our goals, ensuring they resonate with the divine plan set forth for us. Just as a wise traveller checks their map to stay on course, we can establish a practice of revisiting our aspirations. This can be integrated into our daily routines by setting reminders or marking our calendars. By doing so, we not only monitor our progress, but also draw inspiration from our spiritual calling.

As we update our goals, let us discern if they harmonize with the path illuminated by the Spirit of God. This reflection enables us to discern which goals are in accordance with our divine purpose and which may need adjustment or abandonment. Moreover, it invites us to explore new aspirations that align more closely with the unfolding of our spiritual journey.

Gratitude and Celebration of Milestones: Upon the attainment of a goal, it is fitting to pause and offer gratitude for the guidance and blessings received along the way. Just as the faithful are rewarded for their steadfastness, we too deserve to acknowledge our achievements in service to our higher calling. Such moments of celebration not only provide a sense of fulfillment, but also serve as beacons of encouragement for our onward journey.

Through mindful reflection and gratitude, we can honour our efforts and maintain a positive mindset amidst challenges. Let us find joy in simple pleasures or meaningful activities, recognizing them as gifts from the LORD. Whether it be a moment of tranquility, indulging in a cherished pastime or embarking on a pilgrimage of the soul, let our rewards be a testament to our unwavering dedication to spiritual growth, success and fulfillment.

Through proper integration of these biblical principles into your goal-setting process, you can pursue your career aspirations with confidence, integrity and reliance on God's wisdom and provision. As James reminds us, our lives are fleeting and subject to God's sovereignty; thus, any plans made must be submitted to His overarching purpose.

Acknowledging our transient existence, we humbly recognize that our aspirations should ultimately serve to glorify God and testify to His power. Just as God declared to Moses, *"And in very deed for this cause have I raised thee up, for to shew in thee my power; and that my name may be declared throughout all the earth."*

Our goals are ordained to showcase His strength and proclaim His name throughout the earth (Exodus 9:16). Therefore, our journey of goal setting and evaluation must be intertwined with prayerful surrender to the Lord, seeking His guidance and wisdom every step of the way.

10

Taking Bold Steps and Embracing Challenges

In the realm of education, many teachers find themselves driven by external demands, often prioritizing institutional agendass over the genuine growth and development of both themselves and their students. As educators embark on their journey, particularly new teachers stepping into the noble profession, they encounter the challenge of fostering organic professional development, rooted in personal growth and driven by a deeper purpose.

Drawing parallels to spiritual growth, new teachers are encouraged to embrace the path of organic professional development, mirroring the transformative journey of faith. Instead of conforming to external standards and mandates, teachers can embark on a personal quest for knowledge and improvement, akin to spiritual seekers exploring their individual paths toward enlightenment.

Just as seekers may engage in study groups or embark on personal research projects to deepen their understanding of spiritual truths, new teachers can collaborate with peers or pursue independent inquiry into areas of professional interest. The ultimate goal remains the same: to enhance personal practice in a manner that enriches the lives of their students, echoing the biblical principle of stewardship and service.

As aspiring educators prepare to embark on their careers, they are urged to take bold steps toward meaningful growth and development, guided by the principle of organic professional development. This approach, rooted in day-to-day experiences and long-term aspirations, empowers individuals to shape their own journey, aligning with their unique calling as educators and servants of knowledge.

Just as individuals are called to actively participate in their spiritual journey, new teachers are encouraged to seize every opportunity for growth and development, shaping their professional learning experiences according to their aspirations and needs. By embracing organic professional development, educators can cultivate a deeper sense of purpose and fulfillment, aligning their efforts with the divine calling to nurture minds and hearts in the pursuit of knowledge and wisdom.

In recounting one of the pivotal moments in his career journey, Gibson reflects on an adventurous excursion through Europe with his wife, a journey marked by moments of boldness and unexpected challenges. As they ventured forth with limited resources, camping beneath the vast expanse of the heavens, they encountered a defining moment amidst a sudden downpour.

Attempting to grill hamburgers amid the relentless rain, they faced adversity that mirrored the trials and tribulations encountered on life's journey. Despite the unfavourable conditions, their determination to persevere symbolized a profound lesson in resilience and courage. In the face of adversity, they chose boldness over complacency, echoing the biblical exhortation to walk by faith, not by sight.

Similarly, students embarking on the pursuit of knowledge, particularly in the field of education, are called to emulate this spirit of boldness and resilience. In a culture that often values convenience over conviction, they are challenged to defy societal norms and pursue their academic and professional aspirations with unwavering determination.

Just as Gibson and his wife pressed on despite the storm, students are reminded that the path to success is often fraught with obstacles and setbacks. Yet, it is through overcoming these challenges that true growth and achievement are realized.

Failure, though inevitable, becomes a stepping stone to greater accomplishments, shaping the character and fortitude of aspiring educators. Hence, the journey of learning and self-discovery is marked by moments of boldness and perseverance, guided by the unwavering faith that even amidst the storm, divine providence lights the way.

As students embark on their educational journey, may they draw inspiration from Gibson's tale of resilience, courageously navigating the challenges that lie ahead with faith, determination and unwavering resolve.

In this journey of personal growth and spiritual fulfillment, setting goals plays a crucial role in aligning our aspirations with God's divine plan for our lives. Whether we seek to fulfill a calling, nurture relationships, or enhance our well-being, goals provide a framework for our journey toward spiritual maturity.

However, the path to achieving these goals is fraught with trials and tribulations that test our faith and resolve. To overcome these obstacles and realize the full potential of our spiritual journey, we are called to embrace a mindset of boldness rooted in our trust in God's guidance. In the sacred Scriptures, we find numerous examples of bold individuals who stepped out in faith, trusting in God's promises despite the odds stacked against them.

In this discourse, we explore the transformative power of spiritual boldness and its ability to propel us toward our divine calling. Boldness is not a manifestation of arrogance or recklessness, but rather a manifestation of our trust in God's sovereignty and provision. It requires us to step beyond our comfort zones, challenge societal norms and embrace the uncertainty of the unknown with unwavering faith.

Just as Joshua boldly led the Israelites into the Promised Land, we too are called to step forward with courage, knowing that God goes before us and equips us for the journey ahead. By embracing a mindset of spiritual boldness, we can overcome the doubts and setbacks that threaten to derail our progress and walk confidently in the path that God has set before us."

Harnessing Courage for Everyday Triumphs

The Essence of Courage: The word of the Lord to Joshua (1:9) stated that, *"Have not I commanded thee? Be strong and of a good courage; be not afraid, neither be thou dismayed: for the LORD thy God is with thee whithersoever* *thou goest."* Courage, a divine gift bestowed upon every soul, lies dormant within us, awaiting activation and purpose.

It serves as the driving force propelling us toward extraordinary feats and acts of valour, capable of reshaping our destinies and those of others. Its potency lies in its ability to propel us beyond the confines of comfort, empowering us to confront adversities, surmount barriers and attain spiritual elevation. Within this discourse, we delve into the multifaceted nature of courage and its profound impact on our daily pilgrimage.

Courageous Living: Embracing Everyday Acts of Faith. In our journey of faith, acts of courage manifest not solely in facing mortal peril, but also in the steadfast commitment to uphold our beliefs, even amidst opposing tides. Whether it be challenging societal norms or championing causes close to our hearts, each instance requires a courageous stance. Through such bold actions, we pave the path for transformation and ignite sparks of inspiration in others.

Nurturing Courage in Everyday Life: Biblical Insights

Acknowledge Your Fears: Scripture teaches us that courage is not the absence of fear, but the decision to act despite it. Just as Joshua was instructed to "be strong and courageous" in the face of daunting challenges (Joshua 1:9), we too must confront our fears with unwavering faith. By acknowledging our fears, we gain clarity on the obstacles hindering our progress and can seek divine strength to overcome them.

Start Small, Trust God: Like the mustard seed that grows into a mighty tree (Matthew 17:20), courage flourishes through incremental steps of faith. Begin by stepping out of your comfort zone in small ways, trusting in God's guidance and provision. Whether it is initiating conversations with strangers or exploring new avenues of service, each act of courage strengthens our reliance on the Almighty and prepares us for greater challenges ahead.

Cultivate a Community of Faith: Just as the early Christians found strength in fellowship and prayer (Acts 2:42-47), surround yourself with a supportive community of believers who uplift and inspire you. Together, we can bolster each other's courage, sharing testimonies of God's faithfulness and standing united in our commitment to live boldly for His glory.

Drawing Inspiration from Biblical Heroes of Courage: Case studies from history often echo the timeless narratives of courage found within the sacred Scriptures. Consider the story of Esther, a woman of humble origins who fearlessly approached the king to intercede for her people, risking her life for the greater good (Esther 4:16). Similarly, the prophet Daniel exhibited unwavering courage in the face of persecution, refusing to compromise his faith despite the threat of death (Daniel 6:10).

Reflecting on more recent examples, we find the story of Rosa Parks resonating with the biblical theme of courageous defiance against injustice. By refusing to surrender her seat on a segregated bus, Rosa Parks sparked a movement that echoed the spirit of biblical resistance against oppression. Her act of courage not only ignited the flames of change but, also inspired countless others to rise against discrimination and inequality.

Courage: A Divine Catalyst for Transformation

In conclusion, courage stands as a divine catalyst for personal and societal transformation, echoing the biblical call to "be strong and courageous" in all endeavours (Joshua 1:9). By acknowledging our fears and stepping out in faith, we align ourselves with the courageous examples set forth by biblical heroes and modern-day trailblazers alike.

Surrounding ourselves with a community of faith, we draw strength and inspiration to pursue bold steps in our daily lives. As we embark on this journey of courageous living, may we draw wisdom and inspiration from the timeless truths of Scripture, knowing that *"I can do all things through Christ which strengtheneth me"* (Philippians 4:13).

11

Growing Resilience and Perseverance

Life presents us with a myriad of challenges, ranging from the personal to the global scale. In the face of adversity, whether it be a setback in our personal lives, a stumbling block in our careers or the weight of a worldwide crisis, it is natural to feel overwhelmed, stressed and despondent. However, take heart! Within you lies the strength to overcome any obstacle through resilience and steadfast perseverance.

Resilience empowers you to rebound from adversity and navigate through stress, while perseverance fuels your determination to press forward despite the challenges and hurdles that may arise. Together, these qualities form a formidable alliance, equipping you with the resolve and fortitude needed to pursue and achieve your aspirations, no matter the magnitude of the trials you face.

Scripture teaches us that character produces hope, laying the foundation for understanding the significance of resilience in our spiritual journey. Hope, defined as a positive expectation for the future, serves as a driving force propelling us toward our divine calling. Without hope, our motivation to pursue a better future dwindles, hindering our ability to fulfill our potential and positively influence those around us.

As vessels of God's love and grace, our resilience in the face of adversity plays a pivotal role in shaping our character and fulfilling our God-given purpose. It is through the refining fires of suffering and challenges that our character is molded and strengthened, preparing us to embrace the fullness of our potential.

To truly grow and fulfill our purpose, we must cultivate a deep understanding of resilience and its spiritual significance. Resilience, characterized by our ability to adapt and overcome life's trials, is essential for navigating the winding paths of our spiritual journey. Those who lack resilience may shy away from life's challenges, missing out on the transformative experiences that shape their true calling.

In the pursuit of spiritual growth and fulfillment, let us embrace the challenges that come our way with unwavering faith, knowing that through resilience, we are equipped to overcome all obstacles. May we draw inspiration from the examples of biblical heroes who exhibited remarkable resilience in the face of adversity, trusting in God's providence to guide us on our journey toward fulfilling our divine potentials.

Consider these insights for nurturing resilience and perseverance in your journey:

By embracing these principles, you can cultivate resilience and perseverance rooted in spiritual wisdom, enabling you to surmount any obstacle that life presents. Seek wisdom from those who walk in the light of God's truth, learning from their experiences and drawing inspiration from their faith-filled journeys. Shift your mindset from one of fear and doubt to one of faith and opportunity, recognizing that challenges are opportunities for spiritual growth and refinement.

Acknowledge your need for divine guidance and support, understanding that it is through humility and reliance on God's strength that true resilience is found. Reach out to your spiritual community, seeking counsel and encouragement from fellow believers who can uplift you in prayer and provide godly wisdom.

Remember the words of the Apostle who declared, *"I can do all things through Christ who strengthens me"* (Philippians 4:13). With faith as your foundation, approach challenges with confidence, knowing that God has equipped you with the strength and wisdom to overcome. Keep your focus on the eternal truths of God's promises, knowing that His plans for you are good and that He will never leave nor forsake you (Jeremiah 29:11; Hebrews 13:5).

As you apply these principles to your life, you will not only develop resilience and perseverance, but also grow in confidence, optimism and joy. Remember that challenges are not meant to break you, but to refine you into the image of Christ, making you stronger in faith and deeper in trust.

12

Harnessing the Power of Faith and Prayer

The culmination of discovering your true purpose lies in embracing the profound power of faith and prayer. Regardless of your spiritual beliefs, delve into the depths of your soul and reconnect with your spiritual essence. Recognize that the tangible world we inhabit is a manifestation of the spiritual realm. As the Scriptures reveal, *"Through faith we understand that the worlds were framed by the word of God, so that things which are seen were not made of things which do appear"* (Hebrews 11:3). Every physical reality finds its origin in the spiritual realm.

The Bible stands as the cornerstone of our faith, serving as a lamp to guide our path and a source of divine wisdom. Regularly immersing ourselves in its teachings allows us to deepen our knowledge and understanding of God. Through the sacred Scriptures, we gain insight into His character, His promises and His divine plan for our lives. As the Apostle Paul affirms, *"So faith comes from hearing, and hearing by the word of God"* (Romans 10:17). Thus, as we diligently study the Word of God, our faith is nourished and fortified.

Similarly, prayer serves as a vital conduit for nurturing our relationship with God. Through prayer, we enter into communion with the Almighty, pouring out our hearts, sharing our needs and desires and seeking His divine guidance and wisdom. As we cultivate a habit of regular prayer, our faith is deepened, and our trust in God is strengthened.

The Apostle Paul admonishes us, *"Be careful for nothing; but in every thing by prayer and supplication with thanksgiving let your requests be made known unto God. And the peace of God, which passeth all understanding, shall keep your hearts and minds through Christ Jesus."* (Philippians 4:6-7). Through the practice of prayer, we find solace, peace and divine assurance, knowing that our Heavenly Father hears and responds to our heartfelt petitions.

By aligning your thoughts, actions and aspirations with the spiritual realm, you unlock a greater reservoir of divine power, transcending human logic and defying natural laws. This divine intervention, often witnessed as miracles, serves as a guiding force in achieving your goals. For indeed, every individual is endowed with a purpose bestowed by God, intricately woven into the fabric of existence. By attuning yourself to the spiritual realm, you align with your divine purpose.

The realization of your purpose is contingent upon your connection to the spiritual world. Many may pursue their goals on the surface level, encountering immense struggles and failures due to a lack of spiritual awareness. Yet, those who embrace their spiritual connection navigate their journey with ease and grace. While adversity may serve as a catalyst for heightened awareness, it is not necessary to evoke hardship to fulfill your purpose.

If you find yourself drawn to these words, you are already on the path to spiritual enlightenment. Learn from the wisdom shared here and avoid unnecessary adversity. Success, rooted in spiritual alignment and divine purpose, unfolds effortlessly, as it is no longer your will, but God's divine plan working through you. Here are foundational principles rooted in biblical wisdom:

Embrace the Power of Faith-Filled Thinking: Believe in the transformative power of positive thinking devoid of toxic positivity as Jesus declared in Matthew 21:22, *"And all things, whatsoever ye shall ask in prayer, believing, ye shall receive."* Maintain a mindset of hope and optimism, trusting in God's promises to manifest blessings in your life through unwavering faith.

Cultivate Mindfulness and Spiritual Reflection: Practice mindfulness and meditation as encouraged by the Psalmsist in Psalms 46:10, *"Be still, and know that I am God: I will be exalted among the heathen, I will be exalted in the earth."* By quieting your mind and focusing on the present moment, you create space for divine guidance, clarity of purpose and inner peace.

Foster a Supportive Faith Community: Surround yourself with positive influences, whether through active participation in church fellowship or nurturing friendships with like-minded individuals. Being part of a supportive community reinforces your faith and fosters a positive mindset, as echoed in Hebrews 10:24-25, encouraging one another toward love and good deeds.

Combine Faith with Action: While faith is essential, it must be coupled with action as emphasized in James 2:26, *"Faith without works is dead."* Take proactive steps toward your goals, daring to step out in faith, explore new horizons and diligently pursue your aspirations.

Harnessing the power of faith-filled thinking with biblical principles, you can cultivate a life characterized by joy, abundance and purpose. Reflect on the truths of Philippians 4:8, directing your thoughts toward that which is true, honourable, just, pure, lovely, commendable, excellent and praiseworthy. Through aligning your mind with the Divine, you unleash the transformative power of faith to create a life filled with blessings and divine favour.

13

Surrounding Yourself With Positive Influences

The influence of our surroundings holds great significance, akin to the power of our thoughts. Just as a change in scenery can uplift our spirits and dispel negative emotions, altering our environment can profoundly impact our state of mind. Consider the example of seeking solace in nature when feeling upset or frustrated; a simple walk can bring clarity and alleviate the burden of negative thoughts.

Similarly, if entrenched in a negative environment, a shift in surroundings may ignite the transformative change needed to align with our divine purpose. Indeed, embarking on the journey to discover our God-given potential necessitates surrounding ourselves with positive influences. Often, those who could bolster our aspirations become barriers instead. Reflect upon your journey thus far, are those around you supportive of your pursuit of greatness or do they cast doubt and criticism upon your efforts? Awareness of others' influence is paramount; if negativity surrounds you, assert the significance of your decision and seek companionship with like-minded individuals.

The biblical principle of fellowship underscores the profound impact of those we surround ourselves with. As believers, our interactions shape our spiritual journey, influencing our mindset, emotions and actions. By intentionally choosing positive influences, we align ourselves with God's design for abundant life, fostering spiritual growth and facilitating success.

Our environment serves as a crucible for our beliefs and attitudes, shaping our perception of the world. When we immerse ourselves in positivity, we create an atmosphere conducive to optimism, motivation and personal development. Positive influences uplift and inspire us, offering the support and encouragement vital for our journey of faith.

Begin by discerning the positive influences in your life, that is, those who embody the virtues and values you aspire to emulate. Seek out individuals who radiate optimism, celebrate your successes and genuinely care for your well-being. Whether family, friends, mentors or virtual communities, surround yourself with those who uplift and inspire you on your spiritual path.

As stewards of our spiritual well-being, we must also be vigilant against negative influences. These are individuals or environments that sap our energy, sow doubt and hinder our spiritual progress. Be discerning in your relationships, setting healthy boundaries to protect your spiritual vitality. Align yourself with those who share your commitment to growth and support your journey toward spiritual fulfillment.

In cultivating a circle of positivity anchored in biblical fellowship, we fortify our faith, deepen our spiritual walk and experience the abundant life promised by our Heavenly Father. As we navigate life's journey, let us choose our companions wisely, for they shape not only our present, but also our eternal destiny.

Cultivate Supportive Relationships: As believers, nurturing and strengthening relationships with positive influences is paramount. Regularly engaging in meaningful conversations, shared activities and collaborative projects fosters a sense of belonging and encourages personal growth. Proverbs 27:17 reminds us, *"Iron sharpeneth iron; so a man sharpeneth the countenance of his friend."* Surrounding ourselves with supportive relationships provides a network of encouragement and support during challenging times. Actively investing in these relationships allows us to be positive influences on others, reflecting God's love and grace.

Seek Inspiration and Learning: Positive influences are channels of inspiration and knowledge, guiding us on our spiritual journey. Proverbs 1:5 urges us, *"A wise man will hear, and will increase learning; and a man of understanding shall attain unto wise counsels."* Engage in conversations that broaden your spiritual perspective, challenge your assumptions and deepen your understanding of God's truth. Connect with like-minded individuals at events, workshops and conferences where you can share experiences and grow together in faith. Surrounding ourselves with positive influences enriches our spiritual lives and encourages continuous learning and growth.

Foster a Positive Mindset: Cultivating a positive mindset begins with an inward transformation rooted in God's Word. Philippians 4:8 instructs us, *"Finally, brethren, whatsoever things are true, whatsoever things are honest, whatsoever things are just, whatsoever things are pure,* *whatsoever things are lovely, whatsoever things are of good report; if there be any virtue, and if there be any praise, think on these things."* Practice gratitude, engage in self-reflection and prioritize self-care habits that nourish your soul. A positive mindset attracts positive influences and empowers you to thrive in the supportive environment you have cultivated.

Surrounding ourselves with positive influences aligns with God's plan for our lives, enabling us to flourish in our faith and endeavours. Choose individuals who inspire, uplift and challenge you to grow in your relationship with God. Guard against negative influences and cultivate supportive relationships that reflect Christ's love. Seek inspiration and wisdom from positive influences and cultivate a positive mindset rooted in God's truth.

By curating a circle of positivity, you create an environment that propels you toward spiritual maturity, fosters joy and peace and supports your journey of sanctification. Embrace the transformative power of positive influences as you walk in faith and obedience to God's will. Therefore, forge connections with those who share your fervour for success and strive for excellence. These allies will provide unwavering support, encouraging perseverance during moments of doubt. Their positive attitudes and beliefs will serve as guiding beacons, propelling you toward fulfillment of your purpose. Though challenging, altering your environment and associations is imperative to unlocking your full potential. Assemble a circle of positivity and aspiration, for they will lead you along the path of divine destiny.

14

Overcoming Obstacles and Adversities

As inhabitants of this earthly realm, we are inevitably confronted with trials and tribulations, both great and small. Challenges are an integral part of the human experience, yet it is our response to adversity that shapes our journey. In times of difficulty, the virtue of resilience becomes paramount, empowering us to withstand the storms of life and emerge stronger than before. In the account from Exodus, it illustrates the unfailing assistance of God in our times of trouble. We find assurance in knowing that God never abandons us, but stands by our side through every trial and tribulation.

As the Egyptian army closed in on the Israelites, God intervened, casting confusion upon their ranks and hindering their advance. Moses, under divine guidance, stretched out his hand over the sea and God parted the waters, allowing the Israelites to pass through on dry ground. Witnessing this miraculous deliverance, the Israelites placed their trust wholeheartedly in the Lord.

God's instructions to Moses reveal His unwavering sovereignty and providence. He commands Moses to lead the Israelites forward, demonstrating His power to overcome any obstacle in their path. Though faced with imminent danger, Moses reassures the people, urging them to stand firm in faith. *"The Lord will fight for you,"* he declares, *"you need only to be still."*

This narrative serves as a reminder of God's divine guidance and protection. Despite the Israelites' initial fear and doubt, God orchestrates their deliverance with precision and care. He leads them through the wilderness, not on a direct route to their destination, but along a path designed to reveal His power and faithfulness. In times of uncertainty, we are called to emulate the Israelites' trust in God's provision and sovereignty. As we face our own Red Sea moments, let us stand firm in faith, knowing that the Lord goes before us, fighting on our behalf and leading us to victory.

As Christians, we anchor our faith in the unshakable truth that God is sovereign over all things and His plans for us are always for our good. Trusting in God means acknowledging His unfailing love and believing in His power to guide and sustain us through every trial and tribulation.

Even in the midst of hardship, we are called to stand firm in our faith, knowing that God is with us, strengthening and upholding us with His righteous hand. Yet, in our human frailty, we often seek quick fixes or attempt to evade pain, only to find ourselves entangled in unresolved issues and deeper anguish. Instead, when faced with adversity, we are exhorted to turn to God for guidance and courageously press forward. Throughout history, God has summoned His people to embrace change, to journey onward and to embrace the abundant life He has prepared for them.

We must trust in His wisdom, knowing that His plan for our lives is filled with hope and purpose. Change is inherent in the fabric of life and dwelling solely on the past or present blinds us to the opportunities of the future. It is in the crucible of adversity that our true character is forged and we are afforded the chance to grow and mature in our faith. Every trial, every disappointment, carries within it a valuable lesson, a lesson that shapes our understanding and molds us into vessels of His grace. Though the path may deviate from our plans, it leads us to a deeper knowledge of ourselves and a heightened awareness of God's providence in our lives.

Resilience, rooted in the ability to adapt and thrive amidst hardship, equips us to navigate the complexities of existence with grace and fortitude. While it does not eradicate the trials we face, resilience empowers us to confront them with courage and resilience.

In moments of despair, when the weight of the world threatens to crush our spirits, it is essential to cling to hope. Even amidst life's darkest moments, maintaining a steadfast optimism and seeking out the silver linings can bolster our resilience and sustain us through the storm.

Acknowledging the reality of our circumstances and the emotions they evoke is crucial, but equally important is setting realistic goals and working diligently toward them. By breaking daunting tasks into manageable steps and celebrating small victories along the way, we cultivate a sense of fulfillment and progress that fuels our resilience.

In times of vulnerability, the support and compassion of loved ones are invaluable. Cultivating strong relationships with family, friends, and mentors provides a lifeline of encouragement and guidance during times of need. Surrounding ourselves with individuals who exude kindness and empathy fosters a sense of belonging and strengthens our resilience.

Furthermore, seeking out like-minded individuals through community organizations and support groups can expand our network of support and offer invaluable companionship on our journey. By fostering meaningful connections with compassionate souls, we enhance our resilience and navigate life's challenges with greater ease and grace.

15

Stepping Out of Your Comfort Zone

Venturing beyond your comfort zone entails embracing novel experiences, encountering unfamiliar faces, exploring uncharted territories and delving into fresh opportunities. Through these endeavours, your perception of the world broadens, offering insights into your place within it. Moreover, such ventures may unveil unexplored interests or fields of study that ignite your curiosity and beckon you to delve deeper.

The Bible often speaks to the tension between comfort and growth, highlighting the importance of stepping out in faith and embracing change. In 2 Corinthians 5:7, it says, *"For we live by faith, not by sight."* This verse encourages believers to trust in God's plan even when it may lead them out of their comfort zones. Similarly, in Proverbs 3:5-6, it advises, *"Trust in the Lord with all your heart and lean not on your own understanding; in all your ways submit to him, and he will make your paths straight."* This passage emphasizes the need to relinquish the safety of our own understanding and trust in God's guidance, even when it challenges us to move beyond what feels comfortable.

Comfort, in biblical terms, can sometimes lead to complacency and stagnation. In Matthew 14:29-30, Peter stepped out of the boat in faith to walk on water toward Jesus. However, when he focused on the wind and the waves, he began to sink. This story illustrates how stepping out in faith requires leaving behind the safety of the familiar, even if it feels uncomfortable.

Likewise, in Matthew 16:24-25, Jesus tells his disciples, *"Whoever wants to be my disciple must deny themselves and take up their cross and follow me. For whoever wants to save their life will lose it, but whoever loses their life for me will find it."* This passage underscores the idea that true growth and fulfillment often require sacrificing our own comfort and security for the sake of following God's calling.

When contemplating stepping out of our comfort zones, we often find ourselves besieged by doubt and fear. The looming specter of failure and the judgment of others can cast a shadow over our resolve, causing us to hesitate. Yet, as believers, we are called to trust in the sovereignty of God and the plans He has ordained for our lives.

Scripture reminds us that the opinions of others are fleeting and inconsequential in comparison to the will of God. In Proverbs 29:25, we are encouraged, *"The fear of man bringeth a snare: but whoso putteth his trust in the LORD shall be safe."* Therefore, we should not allow the fear of judgment or failure to dictate our decisions, but instead, place our trust in the guidance and provision of the Almighty.

Moreover, failure, though daunting, is not to be feared, but embraced as an opportunity for growth and learning. In James 1:2-4, we are reminded, *"My brethren, count it all joy when ye fall into divers temptations; Knowing this, that the trying of your faith worketh patience. But let patience (perseverance) have her perfect work, that ye may be perfect and entire, wanting nothing."* Even in the face of setbacks, we can take comfort in the knowledge that God is using our experiences to shape us into stronger, more resilient individuals.

As parents, we have a responsibility to lead by example, demonstrating to our children the importance of courageously pursuing our dreams and aspirations. Just as we desire for our children to seize every opportunity to fulfill their potential, so too should we strive to live boldly and authentically, unbound by the constraints of our comfort zones. While stepping out of our comfort zones may evoke feelings of anxiety and uncertainty, we can take solace in the promise of God's guidance and provision. As we entrust our fears and apprehensions to Him, He will lead us on a path of growth, discovery, and fulfillment.

The concept of the comfort zone, the space where we feel most secure and at ease, is a familiar aspect of human behaviour. Within this zone, we operate without feeling overwhelmed by anxiety, utilizing familiar behaviours to maintain a consistent level of performance. However, growth and development often require us to venture beyond the confines of this comfort zone. In Scripture, we find numerous examples of individuals who were called to step out in faith, leaving behind the safety of their familiar surroundings.

Abraham, for instance, was instructed by God to leave his homeland and journey to a land that God would show him (Genesis 12:1). Similarly, Moses was called to confront Pharaoh and lead the Israelites out of Egypt, despite his initial reluctance and fear (Exodus 3-4).

Stepping out of our comfort zones involves taking risks and embracing uncertainty, but it is through these challenges that we experience growth and true transformation. In Matthew 14:29-31, we see Peter stepping out of the boat to walk on water toward Jesus. Though he initially faltered due to fear, Jesus reached out and caught him, teaching him a powerful lesson about the importance of faith and courage.

Personal growth is indeed a journey, characterized by moments of uncertainty and risk. It requires a willingness to embrace change and face challenges head-on. As believers, we are called to trust in God's guidance and provision, knowing that He will never leave us nor forsake us (Deuteronomy 31:6). Success in this journey is not merely a destination, but an ongoing process of becoming the individuals God has called us to be.

As we step out in faith and obedience, we can rest assured that God is with us every step of the way, guiding us toward the fulfillment of our potential. Stepping outside of our comfort zones aligns with biblical teachings on personal growth and spiritual development. In the Bible, numerous passages emphasize the importance of self-integrity, self-efficacy and a growth mindset.

Self-Integrity and Self-Efficacy: The Bible teaches that God has equipped each person with unique gifts and abilities (Romans 12:6). Stepping outside of our comfort zones allows us to discover and develop these gifts, leading to greater self-integrity and self-efficacy. For example, in 2 Timothy 1:7, it says, *"For God hath not given us the spirit of fear; but of power, and of love, and of a sound mind."* By relying on God's strength and guidance, we can overcome challenges and grow in confidence, knowing that He has equipped us for the tasks ahead.

Growth Mindset: The concept of a growth mindset aligns with biblical principles of faith and perseverance. In James 1:2-4, it says, *"My brethren, count it all joy when ye fall into divers temptations; Knowing this, that the trying of your faith worketh patience."* This passage emphasizes the importance of embracing challenges as opportunities for growth and development. Just as individuals with a growth mindset believe in their ability to grow and expand, Christians trust in God's transformative power to shape them into His likeness.

Reduced Regret: In biblical teachings, regret often stems from missed opportunities to follow God's guidance and fulfill His purposes. In Matthew 25:25-26, Jesus shares a parable about the servant who buried his talent instead of investing it, leading to regret. Similarly, James 4:17 reminds us, *"Therefore to him that knoweth to do good, and doeth it not, to him it is sin."* Stepping outside of our comfort zones aligns with God's call to seize opportunities and use our gifts for His glory, reducing the regret of missed chances to serve and grow in Him.

Resilience and Antifragility: The Bible frequently speaks about the importance of resilience and strength in adversity. Romans 5:3-5 declares, *"And not only so, but we glory in tribulations also: knowing that tribulation worketh patience; And patience, experience; and experience, hope: And hope maketh not ashamed; because the love of God is shed* *abroad in our hearts by the Holy Ghost which is given unto us."* This passage highlights how challenges can strengthen our faith and character, making us more resilient. Like antifragility, believers grow stronger through trials, not merely enduring, but thriving in the face of adversity.

Self-Actualization: Self-actualization or fulfilling one's full potential, resonates with biblical principles of stewardship and spiritual growth. In Ephesians 2:10, it says, *"For we are his workmanship, created in Christ Jesus unto good works, which God hath before ordained that we should walk in them."*

Stepping outside of our comfort zones allows us to discover and fulfill the purposes God has ordained for us, maximizing our God-given potential and becoming the individuals He designed us to be. As we align our lives with His will and venture into new opportunities, we experience transformation and self-actualization in Him.

Stepping outside of our comfort zones is not only a practical approach to personal growth, but also a spiritual discipline that strengthens our faith and reliance on God. As we push beyond our limits and embrace new experiences, we cultivate a deeper understanding of ourselves and our Creator, recognizing that our true potential is found in Him.

16

Developing a Positive Self-Image

The initial four recommendations revolve around replacing detrimental thoughts and behaviours with positive, constructive ones, drawing from sound biblical principles. Begin by seeking God's guidance to perceive yourself as He does which is found to be profoundly transformative.

Rather than relying solely on human counsel, God's perspective offers unparalleled insight into our true worth. Learn to reject destructive thought patterns by anchoring yourself in truth, a process that reshapes your thinking. Reflect on what triggers these harmful thoughts, pinpointing the circumstances that predispose you to them and understanding their ramifications. By identifying the root cause, you can pre-emptively address these issues.

Authentic change springs from embracing and internalizing the truths found in God's Word exemplified in passages like Philippians 3:17-21. This transformation is palpable through shifts in attitude and behaviour. Cultivating a healthy self-perception amid a culture rife with comparison and criticism is a formidable task.

Our self-perception is shaped by various factors, some within our control and others beyond it. Overcoming negative influences, whether rooted in past experiences or current circumstances, is challenging. Yet, fostering a positive self-image yields success and contentment, while a negative one breeds feelings of inadequacy and undermines confidence.

Developing self-confidence and self-esteem is a journey that requires nurturing qualities deeply rooted in biblical principles, self-love, self-respect, and self-care. There are moments when doubts creep in, and we feel undeserving, unworthy of the blessings bestowed upon us. These moments of self-doubt can lead us to diminish our own worth and resign ourselves to a life devoid of success.

In our Christian walk, various obstacles may hinder our growth. Past failures may haunt us, instilling fear of the unknown and shackling us to destructive habits and thought patterns. Despite, these impediments prevent us from realizing our full potential in God's plan for our lives. Before we can fully embrace our divine purpose, we must first grasp our identity in Christ Jesus. Low self-esteem breeds a host of spiritual and emotional challenges:

Insecurity: When we fail to recognize our inherent worth as children of God, insecurity and hopelessness can take root in our hearts, hindering our ability to trust in His unfailing love.

Jealousy: Doubting our own worth, we may find ourselves envious of those who seem to excel, fostering bitterness and resentment rather than celebrating the successes of others.

Anger: Comparison often leads to feelings of anger and resentment, as we perceive ourselves as lacking in comparison to others, failing to appreciate the unique gifts and calling placed upon our lives by God.

Fear: Concealing our true selves due to feelings of inadequacy, we may harbour hidden fears of rejection or exposure, preventing us from fully embracing our identity in Christ and stepping into the abundant life He offers.

Selfishness: A lack of self-esteem can lead to self-absorption, focusing solely on our own needs and desires at the expense of serving others and living out the sacrificial love exemplified by Christ.

Guilt: Dwelling on past failures without seeking forgiveness can lead to overwhelming guilt and a sense of defeat, hindering our ability to experience the freedom and grace found in Christ's redemptive work on the cross.

To overcome these challenges, we must ground our identity in the unshakable truth of God's Word, embracing the love and acceptance He offers us as His beloved children. Through prayer, Scripture study and fellowship with fellow believers, we can begin to cultivate a deep sense of self-worth rooted in our identity as cherished creations of a loving and gracious God.

Lacking confidence plunges us into a cycle of negativity and anxiety, inhibiting our ability to embrace the present moment and pursue our dreams with boldness. It entraps us in a state of restlessness, hindering our progress and stifling our potential.

However, by nurturing confidence and self-esteem, we unlock the door to greater freedom, a freedom that empowers us to take bold risks, explore new horizons, and embrace a life filled with joy and purpose.

This journey begins with acknowledging our worth in God's eyes and cultivating a deep-seated confidence rooted in His unconditional love and acceptance.

Never doubt yourself, for God has never doubted you. Even if others doubt your abilities, prove them wrong and astonish them with your success. Remember, you are a cherished child of God, imbued with strength, confidence and greatness.

In moments of uncertainty and adversity, draw strength from the timeless wisdom of Scripture:

Isaiah 43:4 assures us of our preciousness in God's sight and His unwavering love for us, even to the point of exchanging others for our sake. Joshua 1:9 commands us to be strong and courageous, reminding us of God's constant presence and support in all circumstances.

Proverbs 3:25-26 encourages us to trust in God's protection, knowing that He will guard us from harm and guide our steps.

Psalms 27:3 instills confidence in facing adversity, declaring our steadfastness even in the midst of conflict and turmoil.

Romans 12:3 cautions against arrogance and exhorts us to exercise sound judgment, recognizing the unique measure of faith allotted to each of us by God.

Psalms 139:13-14 celebrates the divine craftsmanship of our being, affirming our fearfully and wonderfully made nature.

Matthew 6:34 urges us to relinquish worry about the future and focus on living faithfully in the present, trusting in God's provision for each day.

Isaiah 40:31 promises renewal of strength to those who place their hope in the Lord, enabling them to persevere and thrive.

2 Timothy 1:7 reminds us that the Holy Spirit empowers us with boldness, love and self-discipline, equipping us to fulfill our divine purpose. Isaiah 41:10 reassures us of God's constant presence and support, strengthening us in times of fear and uncertainty.

As you navigate life's challenges, cling to these promises and let them guide you in embracing your true identity and purpose as a beloved child of God. Here are some practical suggestions rooted in biblical principles for cultivating a healthy self-image:

Embrace a balanced perspective on yourself: Acknowledge the reality of sin in your nature, but never forget the transformative power of your new nature in Christ.

Foster a spirit of repentance and maintain a Christ-like attitude: Cultivate humility and seek forgiveness readily, striving to embody the mind of Christ in all aspects of your life.

Respond to divine revelation with obedience: When God reveals His truth to you, respond with action, walking in the light He provides and aligning your life with His will.

Reject negative thought patterns: Refuse to condemn yourself or dwell on thoughts that diminish your worth in God's eyes; instead, focus on the truth of your identity as a beloved child of God.

Acknowledge your limitations without self-condemnation: Be honest about your shortcomings without shouldering the weight of blame for every mistake or imperfection.

Fix your thoughts on Christ and others: Shift your focus away from self-centeredness and toward Christlikeness, prioritizing the needs and well-being of others above your own.

Care for your physical well-being: Attend to your physical health without becoming consumed by appearance or vanity, recognizing your body as a temple of the Holy Spirit.

Pursue lifelong learning with humility: Continuously seek knowledge and growth, but guard against pride by maintaining a posture of humility and openness to correction.

Gratefully acknowledge God's gifts and talents: Recognize and appreciate the unique ways in which God has gifted you while avoiding arrogance or looking down on others who may possess different abilities.

Embrace your weaknesses as opportunities for dependence on God: Rather than despising your weaknesses, view them as reminders of your ongoing need for God's strength and grace in your life. By incorporating these principles into your daily life, you can nurture a healthy self-image grounded in the truth of God's Word and His unfailing love for you.

17

Nurturing Your Spiritual Gifts

Sincerity is crucial in the utilization of spiritual gifts, as emphasized by Paul's counsel to Timothy regarding the rekindling of his gift. While these gifts are divinely bestowed and inherently powerful, their activation and effectiveness depend on the believer's willingness and commitment.

Timothy's fear had led him to neglect his gift, squandering its potential. He must recognize his gift as a divine empowerment, enabling him to surpass his own limitations through the strength of God. The discovery of spiritual gifts often brings about excitement and joy, signaling the Holy Spirit's active involvement. However, it is imperative to acknowledge that the Spirit's work requires our cooperation and initiative. Neglecting to exercise our gifts can hinder the Spirit's work and diminish their impact, reducing them from a blazing flame to a mere flicker.

When individuals discern their spiritual gifts and grasp their intended purpose in serving others, they find profound fulfillment and joy. To foster and develop these gifts, whether newly discovered or long-utilized, Paul provides six guiding directives:

Stir up the Gift: Actively cultivate and stir up the spiritual gifts within you, refusing to allow fear or complacency to smother their flame.

Fan into Flame: Nurture and fan the flames of your gifts, allowing them to burn brightly through continuous practice and dedication.

Guard the Deposit: Safeguard the precious deposit of spiritual gifts entrusted to you, protecting them from neglect or misuse.

Be Diligent: Exercise diligence in using your gifts, recognizing the responsibility and privilege that come with them.

Strengthen Yourself: Strengthen yourself in the Lord, drawing upon His strength and guidance to effectively employ your gifts for His glory.

Do Not Neglect: Above all, do not neglect the gifts bestowed upon you, rather, nurture them faithfully and wholeheartedly for the edification of the body of Christ. By adhering to these directives, believers can unleash the full potential of their spiritual gifts, bringing about transformation and blessing in both their lives and the lives of others.

18

Fostering Your Talents: A Spiritual Journey

"Every good gift and every perfect gift is from above, and cometh down from the Father of lights, with whom is no variableness, neither shadow of turning" (James 1:17).

This refers to the process of actively developing and enhancing your natural abilities, skills and strengths. Cultivating your talents involves recognizing your unique gifts and actively working to improve and refine them over time. This may involve practicing, learning new techniques, seeking feedback and continuously challenging yourself to grow and expand your abilities.

Nurturing your talents involves taking care of your skills and abilities by providing them with the necessary support, resources and opportunities for growth. This may include investing time and effort into honing your talents, seeking out mentorship and guidance and creating a supportive environment that allows your talents to flourish. James 1:17 beautifully encapsulates a profound truth about the nature of God's benevolence and consistency.

It declares that every good and perfect gift originates from the heavenly realms and descends from the Father of lights, Who is characterized by unwavering constancy and boundless generosity. This verse emphasizes the divine origin of all that is good and perfect in our lives. It directs our attention upward, reminding us that every blessing, every talent, every provision we receive is ultimately a manifestation of God's grace and goodness.

Whether it be tangible gifts such as material possessions or opportunities or intangible blessings such as love, peace or wisdom, all originate from the boundless abundance of God's heavenly storehouse. The imagery of the "Father of lights" underscores God's role as the ultimate source of illumination and enlightenment. He is the source of all truth, wisdom and goodness, shining forth with radiant grace and love. In Him, there is no darkness, no deceit and no variation. Unlike the shifting shadows of earthly blessings, God's gifts are steadfast and enduring, reflecting His unchanging character and unfailing love.

Furthermore, the phrase "no variableness, neither shadow of turning" highlights God's immutability and faithfulness. Unlike the transient nature of earthly gifts which may fluctuate or diminish over time, God's blessings remain constant and unchanging. His love for us is unwavering, His promises are sure and His provision is unfailing. In a world marked by uncertainty and flux, God stands as the immutable anchor of our souls, offering us a secure foundation upon which to build our lives.

Therefore, James 1:17 invites us to recognize and acknowledge the divine origin of every good and perfect gift in our lives. In this process, you can maximize your potential, achieve greater success and ultimately fulfill your goals and aspirations. It requires dedication, commitment and a willingness to continuously learn and grow in order to reach your full potential and make a positive impact in your chosen field or area of expertise.

In 1 Corinthians 12, the Apostle Paul draws a profound analogy, likening the diverse members of the body of Christ to various parts of a human body. Just as each part serves a distinct function, so too do our talents and spiritual gifts. Despite their differences, all are indispensable components of the divine design, essential for the holistic functioning of the body.

Scripture exhorts believers to be faithful stewards of the gifts bestowed upon them by God. By employing our talents in service to the divine purpose, we not only find fulfillment, but also become vessels of God's love and grace in the world. Each of us is endowed with unique gifts and it is through the faithful application of these gifts that we manifest the glory of God. Whether gifted in teaching, artistic expression, hospitality or culinary arts, we are called to utilize our talents for the edification of the body of Christ and the proclamation of His Kingdom.

Practical expressions of our talents vary, encompassing diverse acts of service and ministry. From teaching Sunday school to creating inspirational art, from extending hospitality to comforting the grieving through culinary endeavours, every act performed in alignment with our divine gifts becomes a testimony to God's presence and provision. It is imperative to remain vigilant for opportunities to serve God and others in our daily lives. While the impact of our efforts may not always be immediately apparent, we are called to trust in God's sovereignty and continue to offer our talents in His service. Whether our contributions are publicly acknowledged or remain unseen, each act of service bears the potential to profoundly impact the lives of those touched by God's grace through us.

Therefore, let us faithfully steward the talents entrusted to us, recognizing that through our obedient service, we participate in the divine unfolding of God's redemptive plan, bringing glory to His name and blessings to His people.

In order to cultivate and nurture your talent effectively, you need to:

Discover Your Divine Spark: Seek within yourself to uncover the passions that the Divine has instilled within you. Your talents often mirror the whispers of your soul's deepest desires.

Envision with Heavenly Clarity: Break down the grand tapestry of your dreams into manageable fragments guided by divine wisdom. Through clarity of purpose, you pave the path to spiritual fulfillment.

Commit to Sacred Practice: Just as a seed requires nurturing to blossom, so too does your talent demand regular cultivation. Dedicate yourself to disciplined practice, honouring the divine gifts bestowed upon you.

Embrace Divine Guidance: Open your heart to the guidance of spiritual mentors and fellow travellers on the path. Their insights are blessings guiding you toward mastery and enlightenment.

Embrace Divine Providence: Recognize that setbacks are not stumbling blocks, but divine opportunities for growth. Through divine grace, transform failures into stepping stones on your journey to spiritual excellence.

Pursue Divine Wisdom: Let your thirst for knowledge be a sacred quest for divine enlightenment. Seek wisdom in Holy Scriptures, spiritual teachings and the whispers of the Divine within your soul.

Cultivate a Spirit of Gratitude: Approach your journey with a heart overflowing with gratitude for the divine blessings bestowed upon you. In gratitude, you find the strength to overcome obstacles and the joy of divine favour.

Nurture Your Temple: Honour the vessel of your soul by nurturing both body and spirit. Through healthy habits and spiritual practices, you fortify your being for the sacred journey ahead.

Unite in Spiritual Fellowship: Surround yourself with kindred spirits who uplift and inspire you on your divine journey. Together, you form a sacred community, bound by the shared pursuit of spiritual excellence.

Reflect in Divine Illumination: Take moments of stillness to reflect upon your spiritual journey, celebrating the divine grace that has guided you thus far. Through introspection, you align your will with the divine purpose.

Cultivating and nurturing your distinct talents is a journey of profound transformation. It beckons you to delve into self-reflection, summon courage and dedicate yourself to personal evolution. Within this odyssey lies boundless reward. As you embrace your innate brilliance, you not only enrich your own existence, but also become a beacon of inspiration and upliftment to those in your midst. Let us, then, embark upon this remarkable voyage united, allowing our brilliance to radiate brightly, illuminating the world with its luminous glow!

This calls us to cultivate an attitude of gratitude and reverence toward God, acknowledging Him as the generous Provider of all our blessings. As we reflect on the unchanging nature of God's goodness and grace, may our hearts overflow with thanksgiving and praise for the boundless riches of His love. May these spiritual principles guide you as you embark on the sacred journey of nurturing your divine talents and fulfilling your soul's purpose.

19

Realizing Your Core Values

Core values are the fundamental beliefs and guiding principles that dictate the behaviour and decision-making of an individual or organization. They represent what is most important and essential to an individual or organization and serve as a moral compass for how they operate and interact with others. Core values are deeply held and enduring and shape the culture, identity and purpose of an individual or organization. They help to establish priorities, set goals and establish a sense of direction and focus.

Core values can include concepts such as integrity, honesty, respect, accountability and teamwork. By aligning your decisions with your core values, you gain a reliable compass for navigating life's choices. This guidance streamlines decision-making process as you instinctively discern what is right and honourable. With consistent practice, this moral clarity becomes second nature, guiding your actions effortlessly. Staying faithful to your core values paves the way for a life devoid of regrets, leading to fulfillment and success.

In Proverbs 3:5-6; the word admonished us to *"trust in the LORD with all thine heart; and lean not unto thine own understanding. In all thy ways acknowledge him, and he shall direct thy paths."* Congratulations, for in embracing this principle, you have unearthed a pivotal truth in your quest to fulfill your divine purpose and unlock your full potential.

Through this process, you come to understand your deepest loves and aversions. Often, individuals confuse their core values with the cultural or familial values instilled in them from childhood. It is vital to discern and differentiate these influences, ensuring that your choices align with your authentic beliefs. Your life journey is uniquely yours and adhering to your core values ensures that you are not merely following a prescribed path, but rather, living out your true purpose with contentment and joy.

To discern your core values through a biblical lens, reflect on moments of joy and pride in your life. Consider what brought about these experiences and why they were significant to you. Additionally, imagine your life without certain possessions or experiences while contemplating what you would be willing to sacrifice and why. Delve deep into your motivations, seeking to understand the desires of your heart and the driving forces behind them.

Core values, rooted in the Word of God, serve as the bedrock of one's character and morality. These values remain steadfast and unwavering, regardless of external circumstances. Recognizing and adhering to your core values is essential, as they provide clarity and direction in discerning what truly matters in life.

By aligning your values with biblical principles, you gain insight into God's purpose for your life and can navigate decisions with wisdom and integrity. Embrace your core values as guiding lights on your journey of faith, trusting in God's guidance to lead you toward what is truly important and eternally significant.

Likewise, discovering your core values is a journey of spiritual growth that can bolster your confidence and enhance your ability to make sound decisions. By clarifying what truly matters to you, you gain a solid foundation upon which to evaluate choices and align your life with God's purposes.

This clarity extends to vocational decisions, guiding you in selecting a career path that resonates with your values and contributes to your sense of fulfillment and purpose. However, the process of discovering your values requires dedicated time and self-reflection. Values may tend to be stable, but they are not rigid and may evolve over time as you mature in your faith and life experiences. At its core, values are deeply held beliefs that shape your character and influence your behaviour. They reflect what is most important to you and define your identity as a unique individual created by God.

Values also play a crucial role in shaping your responses to various situations and in setting meaningful goals. For instance, your definition of success may shift over time, leading you to prioritize different aspects of life such as family, relationships or spiritual growth. As your values evolve, it is essential to periodically reassess and realign them with your current life circumstances and spiritual journey. This ongoing process ensures that you remain grounded in your faith and true to yourself, even as external pressures and priorities change.

By engaging in regular self-examination and reflection, you cultivate a deeper understanding of your values and their significance in guiding your life choices. Through prayer and meditation on God's Word, you can discern His will and align your values with His eternal truths, finding fulfillment and purpose in living out His plan for your life.

Strategies to discover your values
Exploring your core values is a journey guided by biblical wisdom and we offer a variety of strategies to assist you on this path. Select the exercises that resonate with your soul, knowing that these tools are vehicles for deeper self-discovery.

Recognize that your core values are not static, but may evolve over time. Return to your chosen exercises periodically to reconnect with what truly matters to you and to align your life with God's purposes.

Tap into Peak Experiences: Reflect on moments when you felt profoundly alive and connected to God's presence. Consider the values expressed during these peak experiences, recognizing them as clues to your core beliefs.

Engage Your Emotions: Emotions can serve as signposts leading to your core values. Create a collage of images that evoke strong emotions within you. Reflect on the themes and values portrayed in each image, discerning their significance to your spiritual journey.

Conduct a Self-Audit: Delve into your emotions and reactions to identify underlying values. Reflect on what triggers your anger, complaints or desires, recognizing these as indicators of your core values.

Reconnect with Your Classics: Revisit the influences of your past, particularly those that resonated deeply with your younger self. Reflect on your favourite books, movies, music or art from childhood or adolescence, recognizing the values they embody. These classics may reveal timeless truths that continue to shape your spiritual journey.

Through these exercises, you embark on a sacred journey of self-discovery, uncovering the values that define your character and guide your actions. As you deepen your understanding of your core values, seek God's guidance through prayer and reflection, allowing His Word to illuminate your path and align your values with His eternal truths.

Benefits of Identifying Your Core Values

Identifying your core values holds profound significance in your spiritual journey, rooted in biblical principles:

Finding Your Purpose: Understanding your values provides clarity on your God-given purpose. By aligning your life with these values, you discern the path God has ordained for you, leading to fulfillment and significance.

Guiding Your Behaviour: Your core values serve as moral compass points, guiding your actions and character to reflect the image of Christ. By adhering to these values, you embody the virtues of love, integrity and righteousness in your daily life.

Decision-Making: When faced with choices, your values serve as a litmus test, allowing you to discern what aligns with God's will and your divine calling. By seeking guidance from Scripture and prayer, you make decisions that honour God and uphold your values.

Career Discernment: Understanding your values facilitates discernment in career choices, leading you to paths that align with your God-given talents and passions. By pursuing vocations that resonate with your values, you serve as a faithful steward of the gifts entrusted to you by God.

Increasing Confidence: Recognizing and embracing your values brings a deep sense of assurance and stability, rooted in the unchanging truth of God's Word. By knowing what you stand for and what matters most to you, you walk in confidence, anchored in your identity as a beloved child of God.

As you delve into the exploration of your core values, may you be guided by the wisdom of Scripture and the promptings of the Holy Spirit, finding profound purpose and fulfillment in living out God's plan for your life.

20

Living a Life of Integrity and Purpose

"The just man walketh in his integrity: his children are blessed after him" (Proverbs 20:7).

An individual of integrity consistently aligns their choices with God's standards, reflecting a life surrendered to His moral authority. Living with integrity entails wholehearted obedience to God's principles, whether in the secrecy of darkness or the scrutiny of public view. It is characterized by a steadfast commitment to truthfulness and sincerity, devoid of hypocrisy or deceit.

Living a life of integrity and purpose involves aligning your actions, values and beliefs in a consistent and honest manner while also pursuing meaningful goals and aspirations that reflect your core values. It means being true to yourself, maintaining a strong moral compass and upholding principles of honesty, ethics and authenticity in all aspects of your life.

Integrity is about having strong moral and ethical principles, being honest and trustworthy and consistently doing what is right even when no one is watching. It involves being reliable, responsible and accountable for your actions and upholding a sense of honour and respect in your interactions with others, while living with purpose, on the other hand, is about having a clear sense of direction, meaning and fulfillment in your life. It involves setting meaningful goals, pursuing your passions and talents and making a positive impact on the world around you.

Living a purposeful life means identifying your values, strengths and desires and using them to guide your decisions and actions toward a greater sense of fulfillment and contribution. The biblical narrative provides a cautionary tale in the example of Lot, whose double-mindedness led to disastrous consequences. Though he professed loyalty to God, Lot's decision to dwell near Sodom revealed a divided allegiance, leading to destruction for himself and his family.

In Proverbs 11:3, we are reminded that the integrity of the upright serves as a guiding light, directing their path in alignment with God's will. Conversely, the crooked ways of transgressors lead to their own destruction. Proverbs underscores the importance of integrity, affirming that the upright are guided by their moral consistency while the unfaithful are ensnared by their deceitfulness. This recurring theme highlights the foundational role of integrity in fostering trust and intimacy in our relationship with God.

Do you ever find yourself admiring those who embody integrity, earning the respect and admiration of others? Their unwavering commitment to righteousness serves as a powerful testament to the transformative power of godly character.

Conversely, the crooked ways of transgressors lead to their own destruction. This verse underscores the transformative power of integrity, guiding believers along the path of righteousness and preserving them from the pitfalls of sin. Rather than envying their success, let their example inspire you to walk in integrity, recognizing that true success stems from doing what is right in the eyes of the Lord. Embrace their example as a beacon of righteousness, guiding you in your own journey of faith and obedience.

As echoed in Psalms 25:21, integrity and uprightness serve as protective shields for those who place their trust in the Lord. By upholding these virtues, individuals find refuge and strength in God's steadfast love, safeguarding them from the snares of deceit and temptation. Integrity holds profound significance within the home where its manifestation is paramount. Psalms 101:2 exhorts believers to conduct themselves wisely and with a perfect heart within their households. Here, the word "perfect" originates from the Hebrew term for integrity, emphasizing the importance of moral uprightness in domestic affairs.

Consider the testimony of Job, who, after enduring immense trials, was ultimately rewarded by God with double what he had lost, including ten additional children. Imagine the impact of Job's unwavering integrity on his newfound family — how his steadfastness in righteousness served as a beacon of hope and inspiration. Through his trials, Job's commitment to integrity remained unshaken, leaving a lasting legacy for generations to come.

When children witness their parents' unwavering commitment to integrity, they glean invaluable lessons that shape their character and worldview. Observing their parents' steadfast adherence to righteousness, even in the face of adversity, instills within them a deep respect for moral principles and a desire to emulate such integrity in their own lives. Thus, the home becomes a fertile ground for the cultivation of integrity, where parents serve as living examples of righteousness and integrity. By prioritizing integrity within the home, parents not only impart invaluable lessons to their children, but also contribute to the establishment of a household rooted in God's truth and grace.

The story of Abimelech illustrates the life-saving impact of integrity. Despite his flaws and shortcomings, Abimelech's integrity spared him from the judgment of God, highlighting the importance of moral uprightness in preserving one's life and reputation. This narrative reinforces the timeless truth that true worth and significance lie not in external accomplishments or accolades, but in the inner integrity of the heart.

Living with integrity entails a commitment to inner wholeness and consistency, regardless of external circumstances or pressures. It is about being the same person in every aspect of life, demonstrating unwavering honesty, righteousness and reliability in all interactions and decisions. By cultivating integrity, believers embody the character of Christ, reflecting His truth and grace to the world around them. Through the indwelling of the Holy Spirit, they are empowered to live lives marked by integrity, bringing honour and glory to God in all they do.

The combination of integrity and purpose means living authentically, with a strong sense of personal values and a clear vision of what you want to achieve. It means being true to yourself, staying committed to your beliefs and principles and striving to make a positive difference in the world through your actions and choices. By living a life of integrity and purpose, you can cultivate a sense of inner peace, fulfillment and alignment with your true self.

21

Making Wise and Godly Decisions

Living according to God's ways brings blessings upon our decisions, as His Word provides clear guidance for our lives. As we immerse ourselves in Scripture, we gain deeper insight into the heart and character of God, understanding what truly matters to Him. This knowledge shapes our decisions, aligning them with His divine will and purposes. Joshua 1:8 instructs us to meditate on God's Word day and night, ensuring that we carefully follow all that is written within it. Through obedience to His commands, we pave the path to prosperity and success.

However, it is essential to recognize that success, as defined by God, stems from obedience to His Word, rather than mere worldly achievements. While godly decisions may not always lead to immediate worldly prosperity, they fulfill God's sovereign plan for our lives, bringing about long-term fulfillment and alignment with His divine purpose. Jesus Himself exemplified this truth, making godly decisions that ultimately led to suffering, but ultimately fulfilled God's redemptive plan for humanity.

In the journey of decision-making, we stand on the firm foundation of faith, knowing that God's sovereignty guides our steps for His glory and our ultimate good. Anchored in the truth of His unwavering love, we find peace in the assurance that nothing can separate us from His embrace.

At every crossroad of choice, we embrace the wisdom found in the Word and the counsel of the godly. Just as King Rehoboam's fateful decision revealed, seeking wise counsel is paramount, for it steers us away from the pitfalls of pride and folly.

With clarity, we discern the whispers of the Spirit amidst the clamour of our desires, trusting that God's guidance transcends our understanding. Through prayer and reflection, we align our hearts with His will, seeking His pathways over our own. Courage becomes our companion as we step into the unknown, fortified by the promise of God's presence in every trial and triumph. With each stride, we cling to His promises, knowing that He who calls us is faithful to sustain us. Yet, in the aftermath of decisions made and paths chosen, we find solace in the virtue of contentment.

Like the apostle Paul, we learn the secret of being content in every circumstance, releasing the burden of regret and embracing the endless possibilities of God's providence. Thus, armed with faith, wisdom, clarity, courage and contentment, we navigate the intricate tapestry of decisions, trusting in the One Who holds our past, present and future in His loving hands. In every important decision, we are encouraged to seek God's direction through prayer and dependence on Him.

Proverbs 3:5-6 reminds us to trust in the Lord with all our hearts and lean not on our own understanding, acknowledging Him in all our ways and He will direct our paths. By seeking God's guidance and waiting for His peace, we demonstrate our trust in His wisdom and sovereignty over our lives.

If a decision lacks peace, it may be God's gentle redirection, prompting us to wait or reconsider. Therefore, let us commit to seeking God's direction in every decision, trusting in His perfect plan and timing. Through obedience and reliance on Him, we experience the abundant blessings and fulfillment that come from walking in alignment with His will.

22

Maximizing Your Time and Resources

In our journey of stewarding time, it is important to recognize the subtle traps that consume our moments without yielding fruit. It is easy to find ourselves engrossed in tasks that, though they may seem productive on the surface, drain our vitality and distract us from our true purpose - the reason we are warned to *"Redeeming the time, because the days are evil."* Consider the scenario where cleaning the house becomes a refuge from daunting assignments. Tidying may offer a sense of accomplishment, but it is crucial to discern whether it serves as a constructive use of time or merely a diversion from the tasks at hand.

Scripture exhorts us to redeem the time, making the most of every opportunity (Ephesians 5:16). This means intentionally replacing energy-sapping activities with those that nourish our souls and sharpen our focus. While socializing may initially pale in comparison to the allure of television, the fellowship and joy it brings can invigorate our spirits and renew our minds.

Effective time management involves a deliberate selection of activities that replenish our energy reserves and promote relaxation. It is not about forsaking leisure altogether, but rather about choosing activities that rejuvenate us physically, mentally and spiritually.

Imagine the contrast between a sedentary Sunday spent indulging in televised entertainment and one infused with physical activity, nature walks and enriching reading or music. Which scenario fosters genuine relaxation? Which leaves us better equipped to face the challenges of the week ahead?

By embracing activities that nurture our well-being and align with our calling, we honour God with our time and cultivate a life of purposeful abundance. Let us, therefore, strive to steward our moments wisely, investing them in pursuits that not only refresh our bodies, but also replenish our souls.

In the realm of time management, biblical wisdom teaches us that the allocation of time is a fixed commodity, bestowed upon us by God Himself. Unlike material possessions, time cannot be purchased or hoarded for future use. Through prudent stewardship, we can enhance our productivity and fulfill God's purposes for our lives.

Understanding our unique capacities for productivity is paramount in this endeavour. Just as each member of the body of Christ has different gifts and functions (1 Corinthians 12:4-6), so too do we possess varying abilities to effectively utilize our time. By gaining insight into our individual rhythms and strengths, we can optimize our time management strategies.

In this journey of growth, we embark on a quest to harness the power of task management. By discerning the significance of each undertaking and aligning them with our overarching goals, we unlock the potential to magnify our productivity. Through the lens of biblical principles, we recognize the importance of stewarding our time wisely, prioritizing endeavours that bear eternal significance (Matthew 6:19-21).

Setting goals becomes a pivotal aspect of our time management framework. As we seek to align our aspirations with God's will, we are empowered to pursue endeavours that honour Him and further His kingdom (Proverbs 16:3). Productivity, therefore, becomes intricately linked to our ability to discern God's timing and set priorities accordingly.

Moreover, we explore the concept of "chunking" our time, recognizing the value of allocating dedicated segments for specific tasks. By adopting this approach, we cultivate focus and efficiency, maximizing our potential for fruitful labor (Colossians 3:23-24). Time management, from a biblical perspective, is a stewardship of the precious resource of time that God has entrusted to us. It is not merely about organizing our schedules, but about aligning our priorities with God's purposes for our lives.

At its core, effective time management begins with introspection and evaluation. It involves scrutinizing how we invest our time and discerning whether our activities align with God's will and our aspirations. This process empowers us to reclaim control over our time, recognizing it as a gift from God to be used wisely for His glory.

Identifying time wasters and energy sappers is essential in this journey. These are the distractions that hinder our progress and derail us from our God-given goals. While relaxation is important, indulging in activities that do not contribute to our spiritual, emotional or physical well-being can ultimately impede our growth.

God calls us to work diligently, but He also invites us to rest in Him (Matthew 11:28). Good time management, therefore, is not synonymous with ceaseless toil. Rather, it entails working with wisdom and discernment, leveraging our time efficiently to accomplish what God has set before us. By prioritizing tasks, delegating responsibilities and seeking God's guidance in all endeavours, we can work smarter, not harder. This approach reflects trust in God's provision and acknowledges His sovereignty over time and productivity.

Indeed, poor time management breeds stress and hampers our ability to fulfill God's purposes for our lives; but as we surrender our schedules to Him and seek His wisdom in stewarding our time, we discover a rhythm of grace that leads to peace, productivity and fulfillment in Him.

In the pursuit of effective time management, we are reminded of the purpose behind our endeavours: to glorify God in all that we do (1 Corinthians 10:31). As we integrate biblical principles into our time management practices, we unlock the transformative power of productivity, fulfilling our God-given calling with diligence and purpose.

23

Building Healthy Relationships

Healthy relationships are a cornerstone of God's design for our lives, characterized by honesty, trust, respect and open communication. Just as the body of Christ functions harmoniously when each member fulfills its role (1 Corinthians 12:12-27), so too do healthy partnerships thrive when both individuals contribute effort and compromise.

Central to a healthy relationship is the absence of power imbalances. Partners honour each other's autonomy, allowing space for independent decision-making without fear of reprisal. Mutual respect fosters an environment where decisions are shared and disagreements are navigated with grace and understanding.

In various cultures, individualism holds a revered position, esteeming personal autonomy above all else. However, for those new in their faith journey, such ideals may seem foreign. Like infants in their spiritual growth, they may struggle to comprehend the value of interconnectedness within the body of Christ. Even among seasoned believers, remnants of worldly thinking can linger, leading them to view relationships as encumbrances to their autonomy.

Just as instances exemplify, some believers remain ensnared by this mindset, perceiving vulnerability and transparency as threats to their self-image and independence. Fear of rejection and exposure prompts them to retreat into the safety of isolation, avoiding the transformative power of authentic relationships. In their reluctance to confront their shortcomings and embrace accountability, they hinder their own spiritual growth and impede the unity of the body of Christ.

Scripture exhorts believers to forsake the ways of the old self and embrace the new life found in Christ (Ephesians 4:22-24). By shedding the protective shell of worldly thinking, we open ourselves to the refining work of the Holy Spirit and the sanctifying influence of fellow believers. Rather than resisting the upward trajectory of growth, we are called to embrace the communal journey toward holiness.

Within the body of Christ, we find a sanctuary for vulnerability and grace where our weaknesses are met with compassion and our sins with forgiveness (Galatians 6:1). Through authentic relationships, we are spurred on to greater depths of transformation, as iron sharpens iron (Proverbs 27:17).

Jannie's encounter with Christ within the confines of a jail cell marked a profound turning point in her life. Transformed by the love and grace of her Saviour, she was filled with a newfound desire for reconciliation and renewal, particularly in her relationship with her husband. No longer shackled by the chains of fear, anger and bitterness, she embarked on a journey of forgiveness and restoration.

Despite when she shared her newfound hope with a fellow believer, she was met with indifference and apathy. The response, "So what? So what?" echoed in her ears, leaving her disheartened and misunderstood. Jannie's frustration stemmed from a stark contrast in perspectives – while she embraced the transformative power of Christ, her friend had succumbed to a mindset of self-preservation and individualism.

This disparity highlights a fundamental truth: there is no room for self-sufficiency in the spiritual life. As members of the body of Christ, we are intricately interconnected, bound together by a divine bond of dependence. Just as the various parts of the body rely on one another for function and support, so also do we rely on our fellow believers for encouragement, accountability and edification.

Effective communication lies at the heart of healthy relationships. Regular dialogue and active listening ensure that misunderstandings are minimized and conflicts are resolved constructively. Instead of assuming, partners strive to clarify intentions and emotions, fostering mutual comprehension and empathy.

Love alone does not guarantee seamless communication; intentional effort is required to cultivate understanding and connection. Practical steps such as setting aside uninterrupted time for conversation, empathizing with the other's perspective and speaking honestly and respectfully contribute to a culture of openness and trust. In promoting open communication, it is vital to consider both verbal and non-verbal cues. Non-verbal communication, encompassing gestures, tone of voice and body language, complements verbal expression and conveys underlying emotions.

Consistency between verbal and non-verbal communication enhances the clarity and sincerity of our interactions. Healthy communication reflects the selfless love modelled by Christ Himself. Just as Christ humbly listened to the needs of others and spoke truth with gentleness and respect, so also are we called to emulate His example in our relationships (Philippians 2:3-4, Ephesians 4:15).

By prioritizing honest, respectful communication, we honour God's desire for unity and harmony within our partnerships. The apostle Paul eloquently illustrated this truth in his letter to the Corinthians, affirming that each member of the body has a vital role to play (1 Corinthians 12:14-27). Just as the eye cannot function without the hand, nor the head without the feet, so too are we interdependent in our journey of faith.

In a world that champions self-reliance and autonomy, the body of Christ stands as a beacon of communal unity and mutual care. We are called to embody the love and compassion of Christ, bearing one another's burdens and rejoicing in each other's victories (Galatians 6:2; Romans 12:15).

May we, like Jannie, embrace the beauty of interdependence within the body of Christ, recognizing that our strength lies not in isolation, but in the rich tapestry of community woven by the hands of our loving Saviour. As members of the body, we are called to contend earnestly for holiness, recognizing that our individual growth is intricately linked to the edification of the whole (1 Corinthians 12:12-27).

Let us, therefore, cast aside the shackles of individualism and embrace the beauty of community, where unity in Christ propels us toward the fullness of maturity and the glory of His Kingdom. The apostle Paul aptly articulates in 1 Corinthians 12:21, we are members of one another, bound together by the unifying bond of Christ.

This profound truth underscores the interconnectedness and mutual responsibility inherent within the body of believers. To belong to one another is to recognize that our lives are intertwined, our destinies interwoven. Just as each part of the body relies on the others for its proper functioning, so do we rely on our fellow brothers and sisters in Christ for support, encouragement and mutual edification.

This concept transcends mere association; it speaks to a deep-seated sense of belonging and commitment. It is a recognition that we are not isolated individuals, but integral parts of a larger whole, united in purpose and mission.

In embracing our belongingness to one another, we cultivate a spirit of humility, compassion and servanthood. We prioritize the needs of the body above our own desires, seeking to build up and strengthen our fellow believers in love (Philippians 2:3-4).

Furthermore, this mutual belongingness serves as a powerful witness to the world of the transformative power of Christ's love. As Jesus Himself declared, *"By this all people will know that you are my disciples, if you have love for one another"* (John 13:35). Our unity and love for one another bear witness to the reality of Christ's presence in our midst.

Therefore, let us cherish and nurture this bond of belongingness within the body of Christ, recognizing that we are indeed members of one another, united in our shared identity as children of God and co-heirs with Christ (Romans 8:17).

24

Engendering Continuous Learning and Personal Growth

In the pursuit of spiritual growth and empowerment, reading serves as a valuable tool for self-education. A person committed to godly wisdom embraces a diverse range of literature, seeking to glean insights and perspectives from various sources. While they may have areas of special interest, they remain open to exploring new topics and ideas suggested by others.

Recognizing the adage that "all readers are leaders," the spiritually empowered individual understands the profound impact that reading has on their ability to teach and influence others. They approach reading with intentionality, viewing it, not merely as a passive activity, but as a means of deepening their understanding and enriching their life.

A powerful reader engages with the material actively, analyzing its content and seeking to apply its principles to their own life. They may revisit books, annotate passages or take notes, recognizing the importance of retention and comprehension. Furthermore, they value discussion as a means of processing and synthesizing what they have read, inviting others into dialogue to explore new insights and applications.

In all their reading endeavours, the spiritually empowered individual remains mindful of their ultimate purpose: to grow in wisdom and maturity and to glorify God in all they do (Proverbs 2:6; Colossians 3:16). By approaching reading with intentionality, they align themselves with God's desire for continual growth and transformation, equipping themselves to fulfill their calling and impact others for His Kingdom.

To fully realize their potential, individuals empowered by God's wisdom are committed to a journey of continual learning and growth. They understand that stagnation is antithetical to God's design for their lives and embrace the concept of lifelong learning as a means of spiritual enrichment and personal development.

Embracing the wisdom found in Proverbs 18:15, they recognize that their growth is intricately linked to the people they encounter and the knowledge they acquire. They approach life with humility, acknowledging that every individual and every experience has the potential to impart valuable lessons.

Like humble students in the school of life, they remain open to new ideas and perspectives, understanding that God often works through unexpected sources to impart wisdom and insight. Their teachable spirit allows them to glean wisdom from a diverse array of voices, recognizing that even those whom society may overlook can offer profound truths.

This commitment to continual learning is not merely a passive pursuit, but an active engagement with

God's unfolding plan for their lives. By immersing themselves in the study of His Word and the wisdom of others, they participate in a self-fulfilling prophecy of growth and expansion, aligning themselves with God's desire for ongoing transformation (Romans 12:2).

In the ever-changing landscape of the 21st Century, the principle of continuous learning finds resonance with biblical wisdom on growth and transformation. Just as God calls us to be renewed in our minds (Romans 12:2) and to seek wisdom as we would treasure (Proverbs 2:1-5), so also does the concept of perpetual education echo the pursuit of knowledge and understanding throughout our lives.

Gone are the days when education was confined to the classroom; today, the journey of learning extends beyond formal boundaries and transcends age or occupation. It is a mindset, a commitment to curiosity and self-improvement, reflecting the biblical call to grow in grace and knowledge (2 Peter 3:18).

Continuous learning equips us to navigate the complexities of a rapidly changing world where technological advancements and societal shifts demand adaptability and agility. Just as the wise person builds their house upon the rock to withstand the storms of life (Matthew 7:24-27), so also do continuous learners fortify their minds with knowledge and skill, ensuring resilience in the face of challenges.

The pursuit of continuous learning is not solely pragmatic; it is also deeply spiritual. As we explore new avenues of knowledge and engage with diverse perspectives, we cultivate a deeper understanding of God's creation and purpose. Our curiosity and wonder mirror the awe-inspiring majesty of the Creator, fuelling our desire to know Him more deeply (Psalms 19:1).

Moreover, continuous learning fosters personal fulfillment and enrichment, echoing the biblical exhortation to seek after excellence and to steward our talents wisely (Colossians 3:23-24; Matthew 25:14-30). Whether we are mastering a new skill or delving into a new field of study, each step of our learning journey offers opportunities for growth and self-discovery.

In essence, continuous learning aligns with the biblical principle of lifelong discipleship, inviting us to walk in the footsteps of the ultimate Teacher, Jesus Christ. As we embrace the adventure of learning, may we grow in wisdom, deepen our understanding of God's truth and glorify Him in all that we do (Proverbs 9:9, Colossians 1:9-10).

Continuous learning is not merely a pursuit of personal or professional advancement; it aligns with the biblical principle of stewardship and growth in every aspect of life. As stewards of the talents and opportunities entrusted to us by God (Matthew 25:14-30), we are called to cultivate our abilities and expand our knowledge for His glory and the benefit of others.

In the realm of employment, continuous learning reflects the biblical call to diligence and excellence in our work (Colossians 3:23). Just as Joseph demonstrated wisdom and skill in his role as steward in Potiphar's house and later in Pharaoh's court (Genesis 39:1-6; 41:39-40), so are we called to develop our talents and adapt to the demands of our professions.

Moreover, continuous learning fosters innovation and creativity, reflecting the divine attribute of God as the Creator (Genesis 1:1). As we engage with new ideas and explore diverse perspectives, we participate in the ongoing work of God's Kingdom, seeking to bring about positive change and progress in our spheres of influence.

From a societal perspective, continuous learning promotes equity and inclusion, echoing the biblical mandate to love our neighbours as ourselves (Mark 12:31). By providing access to education and training opportunities for all individuals, regardless of their background or circumstances, we uphold the inherent value and dignity of every person as bearers of God's image (Genesis 1:27).

Continuous learning is a testament to our commitment to growth and transformation in Christ. As we journey through life, may we embrace the opportunity to deepen our understanding of God's truth, develop our skills and talents and contribute meaningfully to the flourishing of His Kingdom (2 Peter 3:18; Ephesians 4:15-16).

In conclusion, let us approach continuous learning not as a mere trend or buzzword, but as a reflection of our identity as lifelong disciples of Christ. By embracing the pursuit of knowledge and growth, we can fulfill our calling to be salt and light in a world hungry for truth, wisdom and grace (Matthew 5:13-16).

25

Celebrating Your Achievements and Milestones

Celebrating achievements is not merely a secular concept; it reflects the biblical principle of giving thanks and rejoicing in the Lord's faithfulness. Throughout Scripture, we are called to acknowledge God's blessings and victories in our lives, recognizing His hand at work in our journey of growth and success.

In Psalms 126:3, we are reminded, *"The LORD hath done great things for us; whereof we are glad."* By celebrating our achievements, we acknowledge God's provision and grace, reinforcing our sense of personal effectiveness as vessels of His purpose and direction.

Moreover, celebrating milestones aligns with the biblical practice of offering sacrifices of thanksgiving and praise. As the Israelites offered sacrifices to commemorate God's deliverance and provision (Psalms 107:22), we offer praise for the progress we have made on our journey toward our goals and dreams. The concept of rewards and celebrations echoes the biblical principle of reaping what we sow (Galatians 6:7-9).

When we tangibly acknowledge and celebrate our efforts, we reinforce the connection between our actions and the positive outcomes that result. This fosters a spirit of gratitude and stewardship, inspiring us to continue investing our time and talents wisely.

Furthermore, taking time to reflect on our achievements aligns with the biblical exhortation to remember God's faithfulness and past victories. As the Israelites set up memorial stones to commemorate God's deliverance (Joshua 4:6-7), we pause to reflect on how far we have come, recognizing the progress we have made and the growth we have experienced.

In our journey of growth and progress, we find echoes of biblical truth in the celebration of achievements, both big and small. Just as the Israelites marked significant milestones in their journey toward the Promised Land with altars of remembrance (Genesis 35:14), so also do we gather as a community to acknowledge the milestones that shape our collective story.

As we reflect on our achievements, we recognize them as threads in a vibrant tapestry of success, woven together by the guiding hand of our sovereign God (Psalms 139:13-16). Each accomplishment, whether achieved individually or collaboratively, bears witness to the faithfulness, perseverance and resilience that characterize our community.

Moreover, our achievements reflect the diverse talents and aspirations within our community, mirroring the rich diversity of God's creation (1 Corinthians 12:4-7). From professional milestones to personal triumphs, each success adds a unique hue to the canvas of our shared narrative, demonstrating the manifold grace of God at work in our midst.

In celebrating both the big victories and the small triumphs, we emulate the biblical principle of giving thanks in all circumstances (1 Thessalonians 5:18). The way Jesus rejoiced with the disciples over the small victories of ministry (Luke 10:17-20), so do we honour every success, recognizing that each achievement, no matter its scale, contributes to the greater tapestry of God's Kingdom purposes.

Our celebration of achievements is a reflection of our gratitude to God, the source of every good gift (James 1:17). As we gather as a community to share in the joyous journey of growth and progress, may our hearts overflow with thanksgiving and praise for His faithfulness and provision (Psalms 118:24).

The Journey of a Thousand Steps: As we reflect on our accomplishments, let us not overlook the beauty inherent in the journey itself. Each step taken, every lesson learned and every obstacle overcome is a testament to God's faithfulness and the transformative power of His grace. In the journey of faith, every moment is an opportunity for growth and celebration, as we press forward toward the prize of the upward call of God in Christ Jesus (Philippians 3:14).

Showcasing Our Achievements: Spotlight on Kingdom Projects - Our community stands as a beacon of creativity and collaboration, reflecting the diversity of gifts and talents bestowed upon us by our Creator (1 Corinthians 12:4-6). From impactful initiatives to innovative endeavours, let us shine a spotlight on the projects that embody the spirit of unity and purpose within our community. By celebrating these Kingdom projects, we bear witness to the transformative power of God's love working through His people.

Individual Testimonies of Grace: Within the fabric of our community lies a tapestry of individual testimonies, each thread woven with stories of God's faithfulness and provision (Psalms 107:8-9). Whether it be milestones achieved, personal breakthroughs experienced or creative expressions shared, let us lift up the diverse accomplishments of our community members as a testament to the manifold grace of God at work in our lives (1 Peter 4:10).

Inviting Reflections and Shared Blessings: Share Your Testimonies! In the spirit of unity and encouragement, we invite each member of our community to share their testimonies of God's goodness and faithfulness in the comments below. Let us create a space where we can celebrate together, rejoicing in the victories won and the blessings received. For as we share in one another's joys and sorrows, we fulfill the law of Christ (Galatians 6:2) and strengthen the bonds of fellowship within our community.

The Impact on Kingdom Fellowship: Fostering a Culture of Kingdom Support - By celebrating each other's victories, we foster a culture of Kingdom support and encouragement within our community. As we affirm one another's achievements, we embody the love and unity that Christ desires for His body, the church (John 13:34-35). In this atmosphere of mutual edification, we find strength and inspiration to persevere in our own journeys of faith (Hebrews 10:24-25).

Inspiring Kingdom Pursuits: Reflecting on our collective victories inspires us to press on toward the goal of our calling in Christ (Philippians 3:14). As we witness the faithfulness of God in the lives of our brothers and sisters, we are encouraged to step out in faith and pursue the dreams and aspirations He has placed within our hearts (Ephesians 2:10). Each triumph becomes a testimony of God's power to transform lives and fulfill His purposes through His people.

A Symphony of Kingdom Success: In conclusion, our community is not merely a gathering of individuals; it is a symphony of Kingdom successes, harmonizing together in praise and worship to our God (Psalms 95:1-2). As we celebrate our achievements, both big and small, let us do so with hearts full of gratitude and anticipation for the continued work of God's Kingdom in our midst (1 Thessalonians 5:16-18).

Together, let us march forward in faith, knowing that each milestone reached is a testament to the faithfulness of our God and the power of His love to transform lives. Here is to many more victories and moments of Kingdom joy as we journey together in His grace and truth.

Celebrating achievements is not merely about self-gratification; it is about glorifying God and recognizing His hand in our lives. As we rejoice in His faithfulness and provision, we fan the flame of motivation and enthusiasm for the journey ahead, knowing that He Who began a good work in us will carry it to completion (Philippians 1:6).

26

Leaving a Lasting Legacy

Leaving a legacy is deeply intertwined with the biblical principle of stewardship, as it involves the intentional investment of our lives in ways that honour God and bless others (1 Peter 4:10). From a spiritual perspective, a lasting legacy extends far beyond temporal achievements or material possessions; it encompasses the positive impact we have on the lives of others through our actions, character and values. At its core, a legacy is the imprint of our lives on those around us, reflecting the values, principles and beliefs that guide our choices and decisions (Proverbs 22:1).

It is not merely the sum of our accomplishments, but the embodiment of our character and integrity which leave a lasting impression on future generations (Proverbs 13:22).

The pursuit of leaving a lasting legacy is deeply rooted in the desire for significance and purpose, reflecting the innate longing within every human heart to make a meaningful impact on the world. However, the biblical perspective reminds us that true legacy begins with discovering and embracing our God-given potential, aligning our lives with His purposes and plans (Jeremiah 29:11).

In seeking to leave a legacy, many individuals inadvertently prioritize the outcome over the process, striving to plant seeds of significance without first discerning the type of fruit they desire to bear. As a tree is known by its fruit (Matthew 7:17-20), so must we cultivate a clear vision of the legacy we wish to leave behind before embarking on the journey of planting seeds of impact and influence.

In the biblical context, legacy is often associated with the transmission of faith and values from one generation to the next (Deuteronomy 6:6-7). Abraham passed on his faith to Isaac and Jacob (Genesis 18:19) and we are called to impart spiritual truths and principles to those who come after us, ensuring that the light of God's truth continues to shine brightly in the world (Psalms 78:4-7).

Moreover, a legacy serves as a testimony to God's faithfulness and grace in our lives, pointing others to the source of our strength and hope (Psalms 145:4). By living a life of obedience and devotion to God, we become vessels of His love and instruments of His Kingdom purposes, leaving behind a legacy that glorifies Him and draws others into relationship with Him (Matthew 5:16). The sobering reality is that few people will witness the full fruition of their desires and even fewer folks will leave behind a lasting legacy that withstands the test of time (James 4:13-15).

Regardless of the outcome, the pursuit of legacy is driven by the universal longing for a life of purpose and significance, a desire instilled within us by our Creator (Ecclesiastes 3:11). However, the biblical perspective challenges us to shift our focus from the pursuit of personal glory to the pursuit of God's Kingdom and righteousness (Matthew 6:33). Rather than seeking admiration or accolades from others, we are called to steward our talents and resources faithfully, using them to glorify God and advance His Kingdom purposes (1 Corinthians 10:31).

The importance of leaving a legacy lies not in personal recognition or acclaim, but in the opportunity to impact lives for eternity (2 Corinthians 4:18). Whether through acts of kindness, words of encouragement or a steadfast commitment to truth and righteousness, our legacy has the power to inspire and transform others, leading them closer to God and His Kingdom (1 Timothy 4:12).

27

Overcoming Fear and Taking Calculated Risks

Fear is indeed a natural emotion woven into the fabric of human experience. *"Yea, though I walk through the valley of the shadow of death, I will fear no evil: for thou art with me; thy rod and thy staff they comfort me"* (Psalms 23:4). It serves as a warning signal, alerting us to potential dangers and guiding us away from harm's way (Isaiah 41:10). When fear overwhelms us, it can hinder our progress and stifle our growth (2 Timothy 1:7).

Scripture encourages us not to be overcome by fear, but to trust in God's sovereignty and protection (Psalms 56:3). While it is prudent to assess risks and exercise caution, we are also called to step out in faith and obedience, knowing that God is with us every step of the way (Proverbs 3:5-6).

Taking calculated risks is not about recklessness or impulsivity, but about aligning our decisions with God's will and purpose for our lives (James 4:13-15). It requires discernment and wisdom, seeking God's guidance and counsel as we navigate life's uncertainties (Proverbs 16:3).

Joshua and Caleb trusted in God's promises and courageously faced the challenges before them (Numbers 13-14) and so too are we called to walk by faith, overcoming our fears and pursuing God's purposes with confidence (Joshua 1:9). Hence, the key to overcoming fear and taking calculated risks lies in our relationship with God (Philippians 4:6-7).

As we draw near to Him in prayer and seek His will, He empowers us to step out in faith, knowing that He is faithful to guide and protect us (Isaiah 41:13). The concept of risk and fear is deeply intertwined with biblical teachings on faith and trust in God's providence. Throughout Scripture, we see examples of individuals who faced daunting challenges and unknown outcomes, yet chose to step out in faith, trusting in God's guidance and provision (Hebrews 11:1).

As individuals have varying tolerances for risk, so do believers grapple with fear and uncertainty in their walk with God. Some may feel called to venture into uncharted territory with boldness and confidence while others may hesitate, fearing the potential consequences of failure or loss (Joshua 1:9). Here are some biblical principles to help you overcome fear and take calculated risks:

Seek God's Guidance: The first step in overcoming fear is to turn to God in prayer and seek His guidance (Philippians 4:6-7). By identifying the source of your fear and bringing it before the Lord, you invite His wisdom and discernment into the situation (Proverbs 3:5-6).

Trust in God's Promises: Visualize success by meditating on God's promises and His faithfulness throughout Scripture (Joshua 1:9). Remind yourself of His assurance that He is with you and will never leave you nor forsake you (Isaiah 41:10).

Break it Down in Faith: Rather than relying solely on your own understanding, trust in the Lord and lean not on your own understanding (Proverbs 3:5). Break down the risks before you into manageable steps, knowing that God is guiding your path (Psalms 37:23).

Embrace Failure as Growth: Understand that failure is a natural part of life and a learning opportunity (Romans 8:28). Even in our failures, God works for the good of those who love Him, shaping us into the image of Christ (2 Corinthians 4:8-9).

Lean on the Body of Christ: Seek support from fellow believers who can encourage and uplift you in your journey (Hebrews 10:24-25). Surround yourself with a community of faith who can pray for you, offer counsel and walk alongside you in times of fear and uncertainty (Ecclesiastes 4:9-10).

In conclusion, as believers, overcoming fear and taking calculated risks are integral aspects of walking in faith and fulfilling God's purposes for our lives (Joshua 1:9). By relying on biblical principles such as identifying the source of our fear, visualizing success through God's promises, breaking risks down in faith, learning from failure as part of God's refining process and seeking support from our spiritual community, we can boldly step into the plans and blessings God has prepared for us (Proverbs 16:3).

Remember, our ultimate reward is not found in worldly success, but in faithfully following God's will and glorifying Him in all that we do (Colossians 3:23-24).

So, let us cast aside fear and step out in confidence, trusting in God's guidance and provision as we pursue His purposes for our lives (Philippians 4:13). For it is through faith-filled action that we experience the fullness of life that God desires for us (John 10:10).

28

Maintaining Balance and Prioritizing Self-Care

Water consumption is indeed crucial for maintaining our physical health, as our bodies are intricately designed to require hydration for optimal function (Psalms 42:1-2). As water sustains life in the physical realm, so does the living water of God's Word sustain our souls (John 4:14).

Neglecting to stay hydrated can lead to various physical ailments, reminding us of our dependence on God's provision for our well-being (Isaiah 58:11). Therefore, it is essential to prioritize water intake throughout the day, recognizing it as a gift from God that nourishes and refreshes our bodies (Psalms 104:10-15).

In addition to water, maintaining a balanced diet is vital for our overall health and well-being (1 Corinthians 6:19-20). Just as we carefully consider the food we eat to nourish our physical bodies, so too should we be intentional about feeding our souls with the spiritual sustenance found in God's Word (Matthew 4:4).

Instead of succumbing to fad diets or unhealthy eating habits, let us focus on nourishing our bodies with wholesome foods that provide the energy and nutrients we need (Proverbs 27:9). By cultivating a healthy relationship with food and our bodies, we honour God's design for our physical and spiritual well-being (1 Corinthians 10:31).

Furthermore, seeking wise counsel regarding diet and nutrition is a wise decision, reflecting our commitment to stewarding our bodies well (Proverbs 15:22). As we seek guidance from trusted sources for our physical health, so should we seek spiritual guidance from God's Word and godly mentors for our spiritual growth (Proverbs 3:5-6).

Let us approach our dietary choices with mindfulness and gratitude, recognizing that our bodies are the temple of the Holy Spirit, created to glorify God in all that we do (1 Corinthians 6:19-20). As we prioritize both our physical and spiritual health, may we continually seek to honour God with our bodies and lives (Romans 12:1).

In our journey of faith and stewardship, we acknowledge that striving for perfection and balance in every aspect of our lives can be daunting, especially in times of trial and challenge (Philippians 3:12-14). However, we must not use this as an excuse to neglect the care of our bodies which are the temple of the Holy Spirit (1 Corinthians 6:19-20).

God calls us to honour Him with our bodies by nurturing them with proper nutrition, rest and exercise (1 Timothy 4:8). When we neglect these essentials, we risk compromising our physical and spiritual well-being, hindering our ability to fulfill the purposes God has ordained for us (1 Corinthians 9:24-27).

Maintaining a balanced diet is foundational to our overall health and vitality, enabling us to serve God and others with endurance and energy (Proverbs 25:16). One practical step toward achieving this balance is to assess our current eating habits and make small, realistic changes toward healthier choices (1 Corinthians 6:12).

Tracking our food and water intake can provide valuable insights into our dietary patterns and help us identify areas for improvement (Proverbs 27:23). Setting achievable goals such as incorporating more fruits and vegetables into our meals, allows us to gradually cultivate healthier eating habits (Proverbs 13:4).

It is important to approach these changes with patience and perseverance, recognizing that transformation takes time and consistency (Galatians 6:9). Instead of seeking quick fixes, we aim for sustainable lifestyle changes that promote long-term health and well-being (Proverbs 21:5).

By starting small and gradually building upon our successes, we can avoid feeling overwhelmed and increase our likelihood of maintaining healthier habits in the long run (Matthew 25:21). As we prioritize the care of our bodies, we honour God's design for our physical and spiritual flourishing (Romans 12:1).

29

Achieving Life Balance: Placing Priority on Self-Care and Well-being

In the whirlwind of our modern world, it is all too easy to lose sight of the vital importance of balance in our lives. We find ourselves swept up in the demands of work, obligations and external pressures, often neglecting our own well-being in the process. However, through my own journey of healing and self-discovery, I have come to understand the profound significance of balance in attaining true joy and contentment. In moments of profound adversity and pain, we discover within ourselves an extraordinary resilience.

This truth became evident to me during a period of intense suffering when I was confronted with my own limitations. It is not the pain itself that defines us, but rather our response to it. Will we allow it to dictate our lives or will we seize it as an opportunity to deepen our connection with our minds, bodies and spirits? Just as our physical bodies require equilibrium to function optimally, so too does our overall well-being.

Often, we focus solely on our physical health, overlooking the equal importance of emotional, mental, intellectual and spiritual wellness. Attaining balance across all these facets enables us to lead lives that are rich, fulfilling and harmonious. As we journey through the trials and tribulations of life, it is essential to recognize that setbacks are not indicative of failure, they are lessons in the classroom of life itself. When we stumble, we must summon the courage to rise once more, brush off the dust and steadfastly continue constructing the lives we envision.

In the rush of our modern world, it is common to overlook the importance of balance in our lives. We become consumed by work, obligations and the expectations of others to the extent of neglecting our own self-care. Through my own experience in self-discovery, I have come to recognize the crucial role that balance plays in attaining genuine fulfillment and joy.

30

Accepting Support: Overcoming Stigma and Seeking Help

When you stumble, rise again, dust yourself off and resume building the life you are called to. Seeking support from others is not a sign of weakness; it requires courage to admit our limitations and make ourselves vulnerable. Remember, balance is not a fixed destination, but an ongoing journey. Embrace the challenges, prioritize self-care and unlock your true potential.

You are not alone in this journey. Lean on the people in your life or seek out those you need. The only limits that constrain us are often self-imposed. Let us break free from these constraints and embrace a life of balance and well-being, guided by the wisdom and strength of our faith.

Call to Action: Pause and reflect on your life, assessing the balance across various dimensions: physical, spiritual, emotional, mental and intellectual well-being. Identify an area needing attention and commit to tangible steps for achieving balance in that aspect. Share your commitment below, fostering mutual support in prioritizing self-care and well-being.

Together, let's cultivate a life that is more balanced and fulfilling. We need to stay connected for further insights and personal growth lessons of life as we explore 'Perspective' and how shifting our view can profoundly enhance our experience of true joy, irrespective of circumstances. Let us pursue a life that is not only successful, but also characterized by balance and significance.

31

Embracing Change and Adaptability

The world is a realm of constant flux where change is as inevitable as the rising sun. Though change may, at times, feel arduous and burdensome, it serves as a crucible for refining our character, molding us into vessels fit for the divine purpose ordained for us. To resist the divine orchestration of change is to resist the hands of the Master Potter, risking the distortion of our true selves.

The Scriptures remind us of the importance of remaining steadfast, yet flexible in the face of changing circumstances. Just as a tree bends with the wind, but remains rooted in the soil, so too must we learn to adapt while holding firm to our core principles and values.

In Proverbs 3:5-6, we are encouraged to trust in the Lord with all our hearts and lean not on our own understanding. This wisdom underscores the need for humility and openness to divine guidance, especially in times of uncertainty and change. When we surrender our plans to God and allow His Spirit to lead us, we gain the resilience and adaptability needed to navigate the shifting sands of life.

Consider also the example of the apostle Paul who faced numerous challenges and adversities in his ministry. In Philippians 4:12-13, he writes, *"I know what it is to be in need, and I know what it is to have plenty. I have learned the secret of being content in any and every situation, whether well fed or hungry, whether living in plenty or in want, I can do all this through him who gives me strength."*

Paul's unwavering faith in God's provision enabled him to adapt to changing circumstances with grace and resilience. In practical terms, this means cultivating a mindset of adaptability and resilience in our daily lives, especially in the workplace. Rather than resisting change or becoming overwhelmed by unforeseen events, we can approach challenges with a spirit of flexibility and creativity. By remaining open to new ideas, embracing innovation and trusting in God's guidance, we can maintain productivity and effectiveness even amidst uncertainty.

Our ability to adapt to changing circumstances is not merely a skill to be honed, but a spiritual discipline to be cultivated. As we entrust our plans to God and remain rooted in His Word, we can navigate life's twists and turns with confidence, knowing that He is ever faithful to guide us.

As George Bernard Shaw aptly observed, "Improvement is impossible without change and those who cannot change their minds cannot change anything." Change, therefore, is not merely an inconvenience, but a pathway to growth and progress that we must wholeheartedly embrace. Let us remember always that our God reigns supreme over the affairs of this world and it is by His command that change comes to pass.

In James 4:13-15, we are cautioned against the folly of presuming upon tomorrow, for our plans are subject to the sovereign will of God. Thus, we must remain ever attuned to the promptings of the Holy Spirit, ready to yield our will to His divine guidance regardless of the personal sacrifices entailed. Sometimes, obedience requires us to step beyond the confines of our comfort zones, to rise to the occasion and follow God's leading.

Consider the Israelites in their exile, confronted with the daunting prospect of leaving behind the familiar and venturing into the unknown. Though the path ahead seemed fraught with uncertainty, they trusted in the wisdom and providence of their God, knowing that His plans for them were for their welfare and not for harm.

Likewise, let us anchor our faith in the unwavering trustworthiness of God's promises, confident that His plans for us, though veiled in mystery, are ultimately for our good. As we navigate the ever-changing tides of life, may we do so with hearts surrendered to His divine will, embracing each change as a step toward the fulfillment of His purpose in our lives.

Flexibility and adaptability are not just practical skills, but also virtues rooted in biblical wisdom. In Ecclesiastes 3:1, we are reminded that *"There is a time for everything, and a season for every activity under the heavens."* This passage highlights the inevitability of change and the importance of being prepared to embrace it.

Throughout Scripture, we see examples of individuals who demonstrated flexibility and adaptability in response to changing circumstances. Joseph, for instance, faced numerous setbacks and challenges, but remained resilient and adaptable, ultimately rising to a position of prominence in Egypt. His ability to adapt to changing circumstances enabled him to fulfill God's purpose for his life.

Similarly, the apostle Paul exemplified flexibility and adaptability in his ministry. In 1 Corinthians 9:22, he writes, *"I have become all things to all people so that by all possible means I might save some."* Paul's willingness to adapt his approach to different audiences demonstrates the importance of flexibility in effectively sharing the gospel. Practically speaking, maintaining flexibility and adaptability in the workplace requires a combination of strategic planning and openness to change.

Proverbs 16:9 reminds us that *"In their hearts humans plan their course, but the Lord establishes their steps."* While it is essential to plan and prioritize, we must also remain open to God's leading and willing to adjust our plans as needed. Developing a growth mindset, as encouraged in Romans 12:2, involves viewing challenges as opportunities for growth and learning. By cultivating this mindset, we can approach changes with resilience and creativity, seeking innovative solutions to enhance productivity.

Flexibility and adaptability are not just about responding to changes in the external environment, but also about aligning our hearts and minds with God's will. As we remain rooted in His Word and open to His leading, we can navigate the ever-changing landscape of life with confidence and purpose, maximizing our productivity for His glory.

Leveraging technology and maintaining effective communication are valuable tools for staying organized and adaptable as outlined in Proverbs 16:3: *"Commit to the Lord whatever you do, and he will establish your plans."* As Joseph relied on his God-given wisdom to interpret dreams and navigate changing circumstances, we can use technology and communication to align our plans with God's will.

During unforeseen events like a global pandemic, embracing remote working tools allows us to remain connected and productive, echoing the message of Hebrews 10:24-25: *"And let us consider how we may spur one another on toward love and good deeds, not giving up meeting together, as some are in the habit of doing, but encouraging one another."* Even in challenging times, maintaining routine and structure, as emphasized in Ecclesiastes 3:1, can provide stability and focus amidst uncertainty.

Furthermore, prioritizing mental and physical well-being is essential for productivity, as highlighted in 1 Corinthians 6:19-20, *"Do you not know that your bodies are temples of the Holy Spirit, who is in you, whom you have received from God? You are not your own; you were bought at a price. Therefore, honour God with your bodies."* By caring for ourselves, we honour God's gift of life and remain better equipped to serve Him effectively.

Finally, seeking support and offering assistance to others aligns with Galatians 6:2, *"Carry each other's burdens, and in this way, you will fulfill the law of Christ."* Just as the early Christians supported one another in times of need, we can rely on our community for encouragement and assistance.

In conclusion, adaptability is not about losing control, but about surrendering our plans to God and remaining flexible to His leading. By incorporating biblical principles into our approach to productivity, we can navigate change with confidence and purpose, trusting in God's guidance every step of the way.

32

Curating a Spirit of Gratitude and Thankfulness

A spirit of gratitude is not only beneficial, but also essential in fulfilling our purpose and unlocking our potential as illustrated in the parable of the man and the tiger. Despite facing imminent danger, the man paused to thank the Lord for the luscious strawberry, recognizing it as a gift from God amidst his adversity. This story teaches us the importance of maintaining a thankful attitude even in challenging circumstances.

Living with purpose and unleashing our potential requires intentional and consistent effort, as highlighted in Ephesians 5:15-16, *"Be very careful, then, how you live, not as unwise but as wise, making the most of every opportunity, because the days are evil."* This lifestyle is not natural, but supernatural, necessitating a deep understanding and practice of living in alignment with God's Spirit.

To live in the Spirit in our daily lives, we must cultivate a spirit of gratitude, prayerfulness and thoughtfulness as emphasized in Colossians 3:17, *"And whatever you do, whether in word or deed, do it all in the name of the Lord Jesus, giving thanks to God the Father through him."* Gratitude is a decision of the will, rooted in acknowledging God's sovereignty and giving Him the glory for His blessings.

Developing a lifestyle of thanksgiving and praise requires immersing ourselves in the Word of God as stated in Psalms 119:105, *"Your word is a lamp for my feet, a light on my path."* By meditating on God's Word, we cultivate inner joy and gratitude, enabling us to maintain a spirit of thankfulness even in adversity.

The concept of gratitude is deeply rooted in biblical teachings, reflecting the divine intention for humanity to be thankful and appreciative of God's blessings. As Psalms 107:1 declares, *"Give thanks to the Lord, for he is good; his love endures forever."* Gratitude is not just a fleeting emotion, but a foundational aspect of our relationship with God and others.

Recent research aligns with biblical wisdom, affirming the enduring benefits of gratitude on our mental, emotional and physical well-being. However, this scientific validation only reinforces what Scripture has long taught about the importance of cultivating a grateful heart. To integrate gratitude into our daily lives, we can adopt these practical habits that align with biblical principles:

Start a gratitude journal: Keeping a daily record of blessings and reasons to be thankful mirrors the biblical practice of counting our blessings and offering thanks to God. As Psalms 9:1 urges, *"I will give thanks to you, Lord, with all my heart; I will tell of all your wonderful deeds."*

Express gratitude to others: The Bible encourages us to express gratitude not only to God, but also to those around us. Ephesians 5:20 instructs, *"Always giving thanks to God the Father for everything, in the name of our Lord Jesus Christ."* Sharing words of appreciation with others not only uplifts their spirits, but also fosters deeper connections and mutual encouragement.

Practice mindfulness of blessings: Mindfulness, rooted in biblical meditation and reflection, involves being fully present and attentive to God's goodness in our lives. Recognizing and appreciating everyday blessings such as good health and restful sleep, cultivates a spirit of gratitude and contentment. As Philippians 4:8 advises, *"Finally, brothers and sisters, whatever is true, whatever is noble, whatever is right, whatever is pure, whatever is lovely, whatever is admirable, if anything is excellent or praiseworthy, think about such things."*

By integrating these biblical principles of gratitude into our daily lives, we align our hearts with God's will and experience the transformative power of thankfulness in every aspect of our being.

Focus on the positives: Philippians 4:8 encourages us to fix our thoughts on what is true, noble, right, pure, lovely and admirable. By intentionally directing our attention to the goodness in our lives, we develop a mindset of gratitude that transcends circumstances.

Volunteer and live generously: Galatians 6:9-10 reminds us, *"Let us not become weary in doing good, for at the proper time we will reap a harvest if we do not give up. Therefore, as we have opportunity, let us do good to all people."* Investing our time and resources in serving others not only blesses them, but also deepens our appreciation for the blessings we have received.

Celebrate small victories: Proverbs 15:23 tells us, *"A person finds joy in giving an apt reply, and how good is a timely word!"* Acknowledging and celebrating small victories demonstrate gratitude for God's faithfulness and provision along the journey toward our goals.

Practice gratitude in action: Colossians 3:17 instructs, *"And whatever you do, whether in word or deed, do it all in the name of the Lord Jesus, giving thanks to God the Father through him."* Expressing gratitude through kind words and actions not only uplifts others, but also reflects our appreciation for God's goodness in our lives.

By integrating these biblical principles into our daily lives, we cultivate a spirit of gratitude that not only enriches our own well-being, but also extends God's love and goodness to those around us.

True thankfulness is not merely about expressing gratitude for blessings, but also about trusting God's sovereignty in all circumstances as instructed in 1 Thessalonians 5:18: *"Give thanks in all circumstances; for this is God's will for you in Christ Jesus."* By adopting a lifestyle of thanksgiving, we can experience joy and fruitfulness in every aspect of our lives, knowing that all things work together for good for those who love God and are called according to His purpose (Romans 8:28).

33

Staying Focused and Determined on Your Journey

Staying focused and determined on your journey means maintaining a clear and unwavering sense of purpose and commitment to your goals. It involves staying on track and not getting distracted by obstacles or setbacks that may come your way. It requires a strong mindset, perseverance and the ability to push through challenges with determination and resilience. By staying focused and determined, you are able to keep moving forward toward your ultimate destination, no matter what challenges may arise.

It involves staying disciplined, prioritizing your goals and consistently taking action toward achieving them. Ultimately, staying focused and determined on your journey means staying true to your vision and not allowing anything to derail you from reaching your desired destination. In the pursuit of our goals, it is important to align our aspirations with God's purpose for our lives and maintain a spiritual perspective throughout the journey:

Clarify Your Purpose: Proverbs 16:3 encourages us to commit our plans to the Lord and they will succeed.

Before embarking on your journey, seek God's guidance to discern His purpose for your life. Your goals should resonate with His will and reflect His desires for you.

Embrace Growth and Change: Just as plants grow and seasons change, our goals may evolve over time. Philippians 3:13-14 reminds us to press on toward the goal for the prize of the upward call of God in Christ Jesus. Stay open to God's leading and allow Him to refine your goals according to His perfect plan.

Maintain Focus and Perspective: Colossians 3:2 advises us to set our minds on things above, not on earthly things. While it is important to remain focused on our goals, we must also maintain an eternal perspective. Avoid becoming overly fixated on outcomes and instead, trust in God's timing and sovereignty over the journey.

Cultivate Spiritual Awareness: Proverbs 4:25-27 encourages us to keep our eyes straight ahead and fix our gaze directly before us. Stay spiritually attuned to God's leading in every decision and action. By seeking His wisdom and guidance, you will navigate your journey with clarity and purpose.

Practice Effective Stewardship: 1 Corinthians 10:31 reminds us to do everything for the glory of God. Evaluate your actions and priorities in light of your overarching goal, using your time and resources wisely to honour God in all that you do.

By cultivating a focused mindset, we align ourselves with God's will and purpose for our lives. Just as Jesus remained steadfast in His mission despite various distractions and temptations, we too can benefit from developing a disciplined approach to our tasks and goals.

In Philippians 3:13-14, Paul writes, *"Brethren, I count not myself to have apprehended: but this one thing I do, forgetting those things which are behind, and reaching forth unto those things which are before, I press toward the mark for the prize of the high calling of God in Christ Jesus."* This passage highlights the importance of maintaining focus on our ultimate goal which is to honour God and fulfill His purpose for our lives.

As we navigate our professional endeavours, let us seek God's guidance in staying focused on the tasks at hand. By practicing mindfulness, prayer and discipline, we can minimize distractions and channel our energy toward productivity and serve God faithfully in our work. By anchoring our goals in God's purpose, embracing His guidance and maintaining a steadfast focus on His Kingdom, we can pursue our aspirations with confidence and spiritual awareness.

34

Conclusion: Living Your God-Given Potential

In Ephesians 2:10, we are reminded that *"For we are his workmanship, created in Christ Jesus unto good works, which God hath before ordained that we should walk in them."* This verse emphasizes that each of us has been uniquely gifted by God with potential and purpose.

Imagine a world where every individual fully embraces and utilizes their God-given potential. It would be a world filled with love, joy and peace, reflecting the fruit of the Spirit as outlined in Galatians 5:22-23. When we align ourselves with God's plan for our lives, we contribute to the realization of His Kingdom here on earth.

Living out our God-given potential is not just a personal benefit; it is a responsibility and privilege. It allows us to fulfill the purposes that God has ordained for us and to make a positive impact on those around us. As stewards of the gifts and talents entrusted to us, we are called to invest them fully and diligently, as stated in the passage from Ecclesiastes 9:10, *"Whatsoever thy hand findeth to do, do it with thy might; for there is no work, nor device, nor knowledge, nor wisdom, in the grave, whither thou goest."*

Therefore, let us strive each day to discover and develop our potential, using it to glorify God and serve others. Let us not wait until it is too late to realize the full extent of what God has placed within us. Instead, let us live with intentionality, seeking to exhaust every talent and opportunity for the advancement of His Kingdom and the betterment of humanity.

EPILOGUE

In the journey of life, there exists a sacred quest—a quest to uncover the depths of our God-given potential, to unleash the true purpose for which we were uniquely crafted. This quest is not merely a pursuit of personal ambition or worldly success; rather, it is a divine calling, a summons from the depths of our souls to align our lives with the eternal purposes of our Creator.

As we have journeyed together through the corridors of Scripture and spiritual wisdom, we have beheld the timeless truths that illuminate the path to discovering our God-given potential. We have learned that each of us is fearfully and wonderfully made, intricately woven together by the hands of a loving and purposeful Creator (Psalms 139:14).

We are not accidents of fate or random chance, but intentional creations, endowed with unique gifts and talents designed to fulfill a specific role in the grand tapestry of God's divine plan. The realization of our God-given potential is not a passive endeavour. It demands our active participation, our willingness to heed the gentle whispers of the Divine Spirit guiding us toward our true purpose.

It requires courage to step out in faith, to embrace the fullness of who we are meant to be, even in the face of uncertainty and adversity. Throughout our journey, we have encountered the transformative power of self-discovery and self-awareness.

We have learned that true fulfillment lies not in the pursuit of external accolades or material possessions, but in the alignment of our lives with the divine blueprint imprinted upon our souls.

It is in embracing our unique talents, passions and experiences that we unlock the door to our true purpose, a purpose that transcends the temporal confines of this world and resonates with the eternal rhythms of the divine. As we embark upon the path to unleashing our true purpose, let us not forget that we do not journey alone.

Our Creator walks beside us, His hand guiding us, His Spirit empowering us, His love sustaining us through every twist and turn of the road ahead. We journey, not as isolated individuals, but as members of the body of Christ, interconnected and interdependent, each contributing our unique gifts and talents to the collective tapestry of God's Kingdom.

As we stand on the threshold of this new chapter in our journey, let us do so with hearts ablaze with passion, minds enlightened with wisdom and spirits emboldened with faith.

Let us heed the call to embrace our God-given potential, to unleash our true purpose upon the world with boldness and humility, knowing that in doing so, we fulfill the highest calling of all — to love God with all our hearts, souls and minds, and to love our neighbours as ourselves (Matthew 22:37-39).

May our lives be a testament to the transformative power of discovering and embracing our God-given potential. May the light of our true purpose shine brightly, illuminating the path for others to follow as they embark upon their own sacred quest to discover the depths of who they were created to be in the name of the Father, the Son and the Holy Spirit, Amen!

Akinbowale Isaac Adewumi
akindewum@gmail.com

Other Books Written By the Author

1. Satanic Attacks and the Way Out.
2. Victorious Christian Living Essentials.
3. Prevailing Prayers of Intercession and Supplication Guides.
4. Satanic Attacks and the Way Out (Second Edition).
5. Principles of Christian Marriage and Family Life.
6. Evangelization and Christian Development.
7. Winning the Invisible War with Christ.
8. Called to be a Soldier.
9. End Time Events.
10. Christ-Centered Parenting.
11. Prepare to Meet Your Lord.
12. Weeds Among the Wheat.
13. Church in the House.
14. Religion or Righteousness.
15. Divine Healing and Health.
16. Power of Praise and Worship.
17. And the Yoke Shall be Destroyed.
18. Remembering Your First Love: *Rekindling Your Spiritual Passion*.
19. Our God: A Consuming Fire.
20. Call to Salvation.

REFERENCES

https://faithisland.org/faith/how-to-identify-your-god-given-talents/

Garza, K. et al. (2015) "Framing the community data system interface," Proceedings of the 2015 British HCI Conference. British HCI 2015: 2015 British Human Computer Interaction Conference, ACM.

https://www.gcu.edu/blog/spiritual-life/weekly-devotional-using-your-god-given-talents